CONCILIUM

concilium 1997/1

WHO DO YOU SAY THAT I AM?

Edited by

Werner Jeanrond and
Christoph Theobald

SCM Press · London
Orbis Books · Maryknoll

Published by SCM Press Ltd, 9–17 St Albans Place, London N1
and by Orbis Books, Maryknoll, NY 10545

ISBN: 0 334 03042 0 (UK)
ISBN: 1 57075 126 9 (USA)

Typeset at The Spartan Press Ltd, Lymington, Hants
Printed by Biddles Ltd, Guildford and King's Lynn

Concilium Published February, April, June, October, December

Contents

Editorial   WERNER JEANROND AND CHRISTOPH THEOBALD   vii

I · The Attraction of Jesus Today   I

The Paradox of Jesus in Films and Novels   3
   KARL-JOSEF KUSCHEL

The Difficult Jesus: Problems of Discipleship   15
   NORBERT METTE

Jesus from a Feminist Perspective: Incarnation and the
Experience of Prophecy   23
   CRISTINA GRENHOLM

II · Jesus Christ – Icon or Idol?   35

The Quest of the Historical Jesus. Some Theological Reflections   37
   SEAN FREYNE

Jesus the Jew: His Interaction with the Judaism of His Day   52
   JOHN RICHES

The Christology of the Primitive Church: The Cost of a
Cultural Mediation   61
   JOSEPH MOINGT

The Limits of Christology or the Temptation to Absoluteness   69
   PIERRE GISEL

Christology and the Paschal Imagination   80
   RICHARD G. COTE

III · Following Jesus Today to God's Reign   89

The Identity of the Christian following Jesus Christ   91
   ANNE FORTIN-MELKEVIK

Kingdom of God, Justification and Salvation   102
    RENÉ KIEFFER
Participation and Witness: The Meaning of Death and Life
    in Jesus Christ Today   112
    EDMUND ARENS
Jesus – Guru of Individualism or Community's Heart?
    Christian Discipleship and Prophetic Church   120
    MARY GREY

The Vision of a New Concilium   129
    DIETMAR MIETH

Contributors   141

Editorial

It is appropriate that the first issue of the new series of *Concilium* should deal with the central question of Christian faith, a question addressed by Jesus to his disciples of all times: 'Who do you say that I am?' At its beginning, and several times during its eventful history, the journal has explored aspects of christology, both ancient and modern. The important changes experienced by Western civilization and the other continents during these thirty years have left their traces on these issues. But what was still emerging only timidly in the 1960s and 1970s has now become quite clear: the intellectual and spiritual balance of classical christology as it emerged from European culture has been shaken by a technological civilization which has become global, and contrasts with a cultural and religious pluralism which relativizes or challenges the relevance of believers' reference to Jesus confessed as sole mediator. At a time when major christologies are becoming increasingly rare (the works of J. Moingt and P. Hünermann are exceptions to the rule), interest in the figure of Jesus is becoming increasingly prolific – sometimes even in an apocryphal way – in art, in the cinema and literature, in many religious groups or base communities and in less academic approaches which prefer the modesty of the story to the universal ambition conveyed by the term christology.

It is impossible to provide an exhaustive survey of these multiple approaches; we can, however, indicate some perspectives which are shaping something like a new set of problems.

In recent years it has been better perceived that the type of bond between Jesus of Nazareth and those who follow him closely or from afar and who possibly confess him as Christ is determinative – from both an epistemological and a theological perspective – in raising the question of his identity. Since there is no such thing as disinterested knowledge, the same is also true of christology outside a certain christopraxis, which can take infinitely diverse forms, at all events more diverse than classical christology and ecclesiology lead one to suspect. Going beyond their conceptual framework, the attention given to the concrete link between Jesus and those who were interested in him allows us to see the relevance of the literary genre of the accounts which contain the question that gives this issue its title: the Gospels are in fact conversion stories which present not only the career of Jesus but also and above all what he becomes in and for those who cross his path.

This relationship has always been problematical, and still is today in a quite particular way, not only because the complex identity of the main figure – indicated by the mysterious link between his name and the title given him – is difficult to do justice to in a creative fidelity which is the essential characteristic of every true relationship, but also because the disciples themselves (or those who could become disciples) are in increasingly differentiated situations which affect their relationship to Jesus of Nazareth. It is in fact this bond which reveals, today more than at any time in history, many facets marked by different contexts or deriving from different types of involvement, extending from cultural or artistic interest to the commitment of one's own existence in a relationship of love.

This differentiation is probably the most evident mark of the present situation, which is leading to an unprecedented pluralization of christ-ologies, an observation often repeated today to the point of caricature: christologies in the Latin-American context of a praxis of liberation; christologies against the religious horizon of Asia; christologies which confront the challenges of individual and collective ills; christologies in a feminist context; christologies after Auschwitz, etc. It is not so much this pluralization which should intrigue us (or possibly disturb the guardians of unity) as the event that it indicates: the departure from 'spiritualizations' or 'abstractions' in favour of the thrust of the human and historical weight of the relationship of the disciples and many others to Christ. Suspicion of the 'universals' like 'man', etc., which have found their way into the formulation of christological dogma ('made man'; 'true man, true God') is only the critical side of a strong demand for respect for the absolute uniqueness of each human career and its place in infinitely differentiated and interconnected social and cultural histories.

The great theological themes of the past (the identity of Christ, his work of salvation, his reception: faith and action, etc.) need to be revisited from this perspective. But this must be done from a threefold perspective: a great respect for the very form of the scriptures and in particular the Gospel accounts; the development of a philosophical and theological conceptuality at the level of the current cultural situation; emphasis on the practical character of Christian faith. It is here that this issue seeks to offer some perspectives.

The first part begins by depicting with a broad brush – though necessarily fragmentarily – the current context of interest in Jesus. These articles cover various contexts and above all present very different types of involvement with the figure of Jesus of Nazareth, who does not allow himself to be reduced to the role that he plays in the Gospels. The second part grafts strictly christological reflection on to this brief phenomenology, linking up with research into the historical Jesus (here at present we are witnessing a third wave), discussing Jesus' Judaism and evaluating the cultural impact of the christology of the early church. Two more speculative articles offer quite contrasting reflections on the limits of christology, which is still threatened by the temptation to absoluteness, and on the place and power of the imagination in the relationshp of believers to their Lord. It is within the imagination – a faculty which is often underestimated but fundamental to the formation of significant relationships – that the theological alternative between Christ as idol and Christ as icon is decided, a choice which leads all individual believers and groups of believers to check how well founded their decision is in their human lives. It is from this perspective that the third part suggests some more practical approaches to the identity of the disciple reading the scriptures and the spirituality of an encounter with Christ, basically marked by the Pauline matrix. A final article reverts to the question which dominates the whole of this issue on relations between Christ and the church, a problem which the journal will be taking up later.

In conclusion, the reader will find an account of the major directions which *Concilium* plans to explore over the next few years.

Werner Jeanrond
Christoph Theobald

I · The Attraction of Jesus Today

The Paradox of Jesus in Films and Novels

Karl-Josef Kuschel

I. The transformation of Jesus in films

The last ten years have brought an amazing rediscovery of the figure of Jesus in German, English and French culture, both in films and literature. 1984 saw the appearance of *Hail Mary* by the French director Jean-Luc Godard. In 1988 the American director Martin Scorsese made a film of the novel by the Greek Nobel Literature prize-winner Nikos Kazantzakis, *The Last Temptation of Christ*. In French-speaking Canada in 1989 the film *Jesus of Montreal* appeared in the cinemas, directed by Denys Arcand. These films are literally only the tip of an iceberg where films about Christ in our media culture are concerned. They are the last in a long series of films including *Jesus Christ Superstar* (1972), *The Passover Plot* (1974) and Franco Zeffirelli's *Jesus of Nazareth*. And at the same time they are top artistic products which portray the figure of Jesus in an independent and creative way.[1] Here is how.

1. Godard – Scorsese – Arcand

In *Hail Mary* Jean-Luc Godard sets the message of the incarnation against the conditions of life in the modern world. Mary, the daughter of a man who runs a petrol station, becomes pregnant, though she has not been with men, and bears a child. Her friend Joseph, a taxi-driver, is at first reluctant to accept the inexplicable events, but gradually comes to do so. Mariological and christological themes are taken up and interpreted in a way which is both stylistically and conceptually independent. The director does not have any blasphemous polemic in view, but wants to offer a film meditation on the mystery of life which is beyond our grasp. For this great

French director, his film is a continuation and a variation of his previous portraits of women in films like *First Name: Carmen*.

In *The Last Temptation*, Martin Scorsese is in search of the mystery of Jesus' messianic self-awareness. Scene by scene this film attempts to explore the question what kind of a figure he must be to whom hopes for redemption attach themselves, who is not afraid to die a sacrificial death on the cross, and indeed who – on the borderline between self-awareness and madness – is prepared to take all the suffering of the world on himself. And at the same time the 'last temptation' of this man is played out fictitiously in a long dream sequence: what would have happened had Jesus avoided his last destiny, his sacrificial death on the cross? What would have happened had Jesus lived a bourgeois life to the end, with a wife and family, dying peacefully, full of years and content with life, and not with the cry of the executed man? So this film is in search of the unfathomable, uncanny riddle of this figure and at the same time attempts to play out alternatives, to break open fixed patterns.

In *Jesus of Montreal*, Denys Arcand adopts another method, without trivializing the offensiveness of the Jesus story. The Jesus of the Canadian metropolis of Montreal is embodied in a young actor called Daniel Coulombe, who is commissioned by the pastor of a Catholic pilgrimage church on the hills of the city to restage the passion play which has been performed there annually for decades. To do this he is to 'modernize' the dusty text of the play somewhat. Daniel gathers together four friends and acquaintances from early days in the theatre, and as they work together the traditional piece is so heavily revised that eventually almost nothing is left of it except the general idea of a drama of stations of the cross taking place in the grounds of the church with a reduced cast and an interplay of action and commentary. The originally didactic piece of religious theatre now becomes a dynamic series of scenes in the tradition of epic and document-ary theatre.

But the piece meets not only with an enthusiastic welcome from the public but also with indignant rejection. Above all the pastor of the church, a representative of the religious establishment, is deeply disturbed and wants to ban future performances. Daniel, the Jesus of the play, thus becomes willy-nilly a Jesus redivivus in real life. That is what is stylistically most impressive about the film: the transition from the role in the drama to the dramatic role in real life, in which each role illuminates the other, from the 'fictionality' of the Jesus play to the 'reality' of what is played out in life. When, for example, Daniel drags his girl friend Mireille, who has to earn money as a commercial model, away from her 'work', he is so worked up about the degrading treatment of models that he drives the representatives of the advertising industry from the room as Jesus once drove the moneychangers from the temple. And the conflict with the pastor also comes to a head. Despite his ban, the troupe of actors begins a new performance. The police are called in to stop the play. There is a scuffle between the actors, joined by some annoyed spectators, and the guardians of law and order, in the course of which the cross to which Daniel is still fixed is uprooted and buries Daniel under it. Severely hurt, he is taken to a hospital, but the casualty department is completely overwhelmed and Daniel gets no medical care. His state gets dramatically worse in the underground station. As in a trance, he begins to address the people waiting for the train with apocalyptic verses taken from Mark 13. With the words 'the divine judgment will come' he collapses. One of his girlfriends offers his body for organ transplants, but whereas his organs give sick people 'new life', the culture industry will also make money out of the spectacular episode from the foundation of a theatre named after Daniel . . .

2. *The paradox: Jesus culture as counter-culture*

These three films point to a paradoxical phenomenon, each in its own way: precisely in its most creative and independent representatives, the film culture has taken up the story of Jesus, and this film culture is provoking a counter-reaction from a culture bound up with religion and the church. The Jesus of culture provokes a culture which is quite definitely opposed to the church and the middle class. Thus in 1984 traditional French Catholics demonstrated against the screening of *Hail Mary* and these demonstrations also spread to Germany when Godard's film came to German cinemas. The same thing happened with Martin Scorsese's film, since faithful to his literary basis, this director had shown Jesus in an erotic relationship with Mary Magdalene during the closing dream. Already in the USA Christians claimed that their 'religious feelings' had been hurt by this film.[2] It was said that in some scenes the borderline of blasphemy had been crossed. Other critics, including the American journalist and Catholic theologian Andrew Greeley, did not feel in any way challenged by the fact that here Jesus desired and loved a woman. The question 'Could Jesus desire a woman?' did not trouble him at all. If Jesus had been a true human being, Greeley argued, he could also have loved a woman. On the contrary, Greeley felt that the film contained a deep religious challenge; it was more powerful and attractive than the novel on which it was based. Although Scorsese's Jesus was not the Jesus of the

Bible, the film prompted one to reflect in a secular culture on who Jesus was and what he stood for.[3] *Time Magazine* also felt prompted by the Scorsese film to raise the age-old question 'Who was Jesus?' again in a cover story of its own.[4]

The reaction in Germany was similarly divided. One of the best known mass-circulation magazines called Scorsese's work the 'scandal film of the year' and had a lead story with the significant headline 'Might Jesus love a woman?'[5] Above all the dream sequence in which Jesus sleeps with Mary Magdalene, has a family and thus refuses to be Messiah, also stirred people up in Germany. Even in more serious organs like the weekly *Die Zeit* there were arguments for and against. Here the reaction of a prominent theatre critic was of particular significance for the secular majority culture in a country like Germany. In fact the Jesus film had prompted him to do precisely what Andrew Greeley thought desirable: after a long time to come to grips again with a figure who seemed to have been long integrated, dismissed and passed by as part of his own religious biography. But this did not lead the critic to identify himself with Jesus and his cause; it led, rather, to a new amazement at what Christian symbolism asks of people: it offers an executed and tortured man as a basic religious symbol. This is what the critic actually said:

> Since I served at the altar, the figure of Jesus has ceased to be of concern to me. Gradually I came to feel that he was unattractive, rather shrill, biased and quite overpowering. When later religious matters came to be talked about, it was usually in Enlightenment terms, and the conversation turned on historical topics or criticisms of culture. I am far from claiming that Scorsese's film has led me back to the path of religious virtue. But it has caused me to reflect on some things: on the truly terrifying symbolism of Christianity (what other religion hangs a tortured body streaming with blood in every school room and every kindergarten?); on the incomprehensible, curious and yet persistently effective stories which are in circulation about this Jesus; and on the fact that 'under the holy fables and guises of Jesus' life lies hidden one of the most painful instances of the martyrdom of knowledge for love' (Nietzsche).[6]

So these Jesus films are products of a post-modern post-Christian culture which runs counter to a traditionally religious culture. As cultural products they are counter-cultural phenomena. They show the time-lags in the overlapping cultures by which a modern society is governed.

The film *Jesus of Montreal* is particularly significant here.[7] The clash of cultures which develops when one seeks to come to grips with Jesus is already depicted in the story itself. The actor who plays Jesus breaks out of the role given him by the church establishment. The story of Jesus, which has sunk to becoming a ceremonial cultic drama, which has been trivialized politically and blunted socially, shows its renewed explosive force – precisely in the face of a traditionally Christian society which thinks that it has finished with the Jesus story. Here the medium of film shares in the contradictions of modern society: it is at the same time both an expression of culture and a protest against culture; it fights against the culture business of which it is a part; it unmasks the mechanisms of commercialization and marketing and at the same time is dependent on them for having any effect.

II. The transformation of Jesus in literature

We also find the same paradoxical structure in contemporary literature.[8] I would like to demonstrate the exemplary significance of the story of Jesus for grappling with present-day culture by means of three culturally different examples: novels from Paraguay, from the former Soviet Union and Portugal. Differences and analogies can become visible in an inter-cultural comparison. Here too the heuristic question is how Jesus – the product of a particular culture – can at the same time run counter to this culture: he expresses the culture and at the same time transcends it.

1. *Paraguay, Augusto Roa Bastos'* Son of Man

Augusto Roa Bastos, who was born in Paraguay in 1917, is regarded as one of the most significant writers from Latin America.[9] His fame is based not least on *Son of Man*, his novel about Jesus, published for the first time in Buenos Aires in 1959, and revised in the 1980s.[10] Critics accord this book the same status as Garcia Màrquez's *One Hundred Years of Solitude*, since in an imposing temporal fresco it presents part of Latin American history, taking Paraguay as its example. It tells of failed attempts at revolution, peasants' revolts, wars which swallowed up peoples and decades of dictatorship. It tells a history of constant plundering and oppression of the indigenous population, of owners of vast estates, and of the majority of the inhabitants reduced to extreme poverty.

Augustus Roa Bastos, himself one of the middle class, writes a novel in the interest of revolutionary change. For him the centre of focus is the ordinary person, the 'son of man', and this figure is none other than the oppressed, mocked, expelled and intimidated Paraguayan people. One motto of the novel has been taken from the book of the prophet Ezekiel: 'Son of man, you dwell among a disobedient house.' So it is about the history of the anguish and suffering of Paraguay, about the power of human beings to resist in the face of their physical extermination and their moral humiliation.

Symbols of redemption, full of poetry and beauty, are brought into this story, like the leprous Christ of Itapé. This Christ is the work of a guitar-playing wood-carver who is sick with leprosy, and it may not be taken into the official church there. So the inhabitants of the village venerate it in the open air on a hill. In this way this cross in particular becomes a sign of resistance, indeed a sign of hope. One of the figures provides the key for understanding the whole novel.

> I think not only of the two. I think of the others who are in the same situation and have been humiliated to the extreme, just like the suffering, tortured human being, always and everywhere the same one, who is immortal by destiny. There must be a way out of the tremendous madness of a man being crucified by men. Otherwise we would have to believe that the human race is cursed for ever, that this is hell and that we may not hope for any redemption. There must be a way out, otherwise . . . [11]

So Augusto Roa Bastos' novel *Son of Man* is a modern novel of the passion, the point of which is a theology of liberation. It not only cuts across the political 'culture' of its land, in opposition to the rulers, passing judgment on the violence of the dictators and the ruling classes who support them. It also cuts across the established Christian church culture of its country. A symbolic sign of this is offered by the rites of 'wild religion' which are taken up time and again. They become visible when the church authorities refuse the 'leprous Christ' entry into the church. Consequently the religious praxis of the people develops 'in the open air'. And this is very close to the cult of the indigenous population, which in any case knows no houses of God but 'direct' contact with the deities. The Christ of Itapé is at the same time both an expression of culture and protest against it.

2. *Kirghizia: Chinghiz Aitmatov's* The Place of Execution

In 1986, in the Soviet Union, which still existed at that time, there appeared one of the most controversial books, which then also attracted great attention internationally: the novel *The Place of Execution*, by Chinghiz Aitmatov, who was born in 1928. The book was controversial, not least because more than any other Soviet author before him the author had dared openly to attack the social problems of the USSR: alcoholism, drugs, the daily escalations of violence. But it was also controversial because the novel – in the tradition of the Russian writer Mikhail Bulgakov – includes in a dream a dialogue between Pilate and Jesus.

The author of this book is himself an inter-cultural phenomenon. He is a Kirghizian and at the same time a product of the multi-cultural former Soviet Union, to which he owes his education, first as a zoo technician and then as a writer. He is a Muslim who then opens himself to the history of Russian Christianity, and he has been awarded Russian literary prizes. He comes from a humble farming background and in the time of Perestroika succeeded in rising to become a member of the Presidential Council.[12] In form his novel is already an intercultural mixture. It has a Kirghizian level (the story of the Shepherd Boston), an archaic-animal level (the story of the she-wolf Akbara) and, for the first time in Aitmatov's work, a Russian Christian level – the story of Avdi Kallistratov, the priest's son and God-seeker who was expelled from the priests' seminar, and in the steps of Christ suffers a martyr death on the cross. In his feverish fantasies, as in Bulgakov's novel *Master and Margarita*, Christ speaks with Pontius Pilate. In this story Avdi, the ex-theologian, is a journalist who openly attacks drug-dealing and is persecuted and tortured by the drug Mafia.

Furthermore Avdi sees the scene between Pilate and Jesus in a vision when, maltreated by the drug-dealers, he struggles with death. Pilate and Jesus discuss the very questions that concern the hero of the book and also its author. 'Jesus' embodies the utopian surplus in all culture and stands for the principle of 'happiness and equality for all men and women'. Here he is the counter-principle to Pilate, the embodiment of an ineradicable cynicism, who is accustomed to mock the rebels and idealists and at the same time to send them to the cross. Kingdom of righteousness? That can never be! That is a fantasy! By contrast Jesus is the human being's dream-picture of himself which always clashes with brutal reality; it fails because of the circumstances but without being refuted.

The dialogue between Jesus and Pilate points back to the story of Avdi himself. He not only dreams of Christ, but is himself increasingly forced by his opponents into the role of Christ. Already before this vision Avdi has mockingly been described as the 'new Christ', who has come to redeem human beings – in this case the drug dealers – from their unworthy existence. Here Avdi is quite clear that the Christian religion, which has been in the world for ages, has not really changed any of the circumstances of the earth. On the contrary, has not 'materialistic science long since driven the aspen shaft into the tomb of Christian faith', if not the 'military superiority', the religion which now exercises sole domination?[13]

Yet for this Jesus redivivus from Kirghizia, the story of the Nazarene still retains its recalcitrant power. In an unculture of brutality and oppression, in a wolf society in which the law of the stronger dominates, the cross works as a counter-force of impotence which goes against the facts. The key passage in Avdi's meditation on Jesus runs:

> And you, Master, make yourself ready for the cruellest execution, so that human beings may open themselves to kindness and sympathy, so that they may perceive what fundamentally distinguishes the rational from the irrational, for the way of human beings on earth is laborious, and evil is deeply rooted in them. Can we attain the absolute ideal on the way – the understanding which gives wings to freedom of thought? And the exalted personality who conquers evil in himself for all time, just as an infectious illness can be conquered? Oh, if only this could be attained! My God, what a burden you have laid upon yourself, to improve a world which cannot be improved?[14]

But like the Jesus whom he sees in a vision, the idealist Avdi also fails, and the Christ-typology which was hinted at earlier is completed in his failure: tortured and maltreated by the drunken hordes, this 'new Christ' is hanged on a tree and is now indistinguishable from his Christ: 'His look recalled one who had been hanged or crucified.'[15] And before Avdi dies, he recalls a prayer to Christ which he learned as a youth, a prayer for 'the salvation of the human soul'.[16]

Chinghiz Aitmatov's novel, written in a completely different culture, is also a novel of resistance. For the problems which it reflects are structurally analogous to those of Latin America. Both novels are about the experience of oppression, violence, power, brutality; in short about the powers of evil which seem to triumph in the world. And these powers of evil stand behind the stories of the passion of humankind, a passion which seems to be eternal, behind the crosses which it seems impossible to eradicate from world history. And yet these 'hells' too cannot refute the real vision of humanity which is embodied in Jesus culture: that there will be a time when human beings cease to be wolves to one another and they recall that 'all human beings taken together are God's image on earth'.[17]

3. Portugal: José Saramago, The Gospel according to Jesus Christ

José Saramago is one of the most significant Portuguese authors. Born in 1922 into a family of agricultural workers in the province of Ribatejo, he later worked as a journalist with various Lisbon newspapers before turning more intensively to writing in 1966, His Jesus novel, which appeared in 1991, follows an old pattern.[18] For in this book Christ appears once again as a figure of his time in a historical context which is recreated historically by the author. Here is a variation on a pattern familiar in European literature from Ernest Renan's *Life of Jesus* (1863), through Giovanni Papini's *The Story of Christ* (1921) and Max Brod's *The Master* (1953). And Saramago also makes Jesus himself speak again. He depicts him as a 'man among men', hungry for life and full of curiosity, delighting in the senses and appreciative, sometimes anxious and uncertain.

But there is one dimension of this presentation of Jesus which radically explodes the traditional narrative scheme. This is the guilt-feelings by which Saramago's Jesus is tormented at a very early stage. How many newborn children has the tyrant Herod killed on his behalf? This question already torments Jesus as a child in gloomy dreams. And at a very early age he is a seeker after truth; for this reason he leaves the home in which he had served as a simple joiner's apprentice. In Bethlehem he lives the life of a shepherd for four years, and then he stays among fishermen by the Sea of Galilee. 'You will receive power and glory', he is told one day in the wilderness, out of a pillar of smoke. But only later does he learn the reason for his tormenting unrest: his life hitherto was a test, since he has been chosen by God.

And here above all the novel focusses on the problem of God. For the element in this book about Jesus by the Portuguese author which is so specifically critical of culture, indeed explodes cultures, is that of God himself as reflected in the figure of Jesus. God's action in creation and his attitude towards his Son Jesus is radically put in crisis. What began as a Jesus novel intensifies into a novel about the crisis of God, indeed cynical doubt about God. The novel of this author from a Christian culture thus denies the culture its religious legitimacy. For centuries this has consisted in seeing the story of Jesus as an expression of the will of God, as a way of redemption and salvation. What happened to Jesus stems from God's gracious mercy and loving care. The novel explodes the way in which these are naturally taken together. God himself becomes a questionable figure, since in his teamwork with the devil he abuses his Son Jesus, so that with the help of this dramatic and effective sacrificial death he rises 'from being the God of the Hebrews to being the God of the Catholics'.[19] Jesus can have power and glory, but only after his death; now he is foreseen as the 'lamb of God', whose death God needs for his universal establishment of himself in humankind. His sacrificial death will not alter anything, since it follows 'a never-ending history of iron and blood, of fire and ashes, an infinite sea of suffering and tears'.[20]

And why is that so? Why does God want to impose himself in this way? That is the primal question of the novel, but it remains unanswered, and neither Jesus nor his disciples can resolve it. It is the abiding riddle, right up to the death of Jesus on the cross, and Samarago's Jesus dies without understanding why his death on the cross must happen.

> Jesus dies, his life is already about to leave him, when suddenly above his head the heavens open wide and God appears . . . he speaks and his voice resounds over the whole earth. He speaks, 'You are my beloved son, with you I am well pleased.' Then Jesus understood that he had been taken behind the light as a lamb is taken to the place of sacrifice, that his living and dying had been predetermined since the very beginning. It struck him what a stream of blood and suffering would go out from him and flood the whole earth, and towards the open heaven, where God was laughing, he shouted, 'People, forgive him, for he does not know what he has done.'[21]

III. The paradox

Literature and film are critical dialogues of the culture with itself. If they are aesthetic and creative, they succeed in denouncing traditional plausibilities in a culture, countering standardized perspectives and exploding established traditions. Therefore great works of art are always an expression of their culture and at the same time resistance against that culture; they are culture and counter-culture. So great works of art always demonstrate a paradoxical structure.

This cultural paradox can be exemplified more than anywhere else in the form of Jesus. For the works of art which are concerned with him are similarly paradoxical to the highest degree: they show Jesus as part of the culture, but at the same time they bring out the fact that no culture can really 'absorb' the figure of the Nazarene. They show Jesus as an authentic expression of culture, but at the same time show that no culture can level down his person to the point of triviality. Wholly an element of culture, the Jesus of the novelists and film-makers at the same time explodes this culture.

This power to inculturate and at the same time to resist being levelled down to the dominant culture is of great theological relevance. For this combination of immanence in culture and transcendence of culture is characteristic of Jesus and the message about him as Messiah of Israel and Kyrios of the world from the very beginning.[22] This power to transcend the culture is an expression of the hope that the cultures – in the spirit of Christ – will constantly prove to be realities that can be changed.

Translated by John Bowden

Notes

1. There is a good survey of the international film scene in *Religion im Film. Lexikon mit Kurzkritiken und Stichworten zu 1200 Kinofilmen*, Cologne [2]1993 (Katholisches Institut für Medieninformation).

2. Cf. *National Catholic Reporter*, 26 August 1988.

3. A. Greeley, 'Blasphemy or Artistry?', *The New York Times*, 14 August 1988.

4. *Time*, 15 August 1988 ('Who was Jesus? A Startling New Movie Raises an Age-old Question').

5. *Quick*, 9 November 1988 ('Der Skandalfilm des Jahres: Darf Jesus eine Frau lieben?').

6. U. Greiner, *Die Zeit*, 11 November 1988.

7. See also the analysis by R. Zwick, 'Entmythologisierung versus *Imitatio Jesu*. Thematisierungen des Evangeliums in Denys Arcands Film "Jesus von Montreal"', *Communicatio Socialis* 23, 1990, 2, 17–47.

8. For the picture of Jesus in German literature up to the beginning of the 1980s see K.-J. Kuschel, *Jesus in der deutschsprachigen Gegenwartsliteratur*, Zurich and Cologne 1978; id., *Der andere Jesus. Ein Lesebuch literarischer Texte*, Zurich and Cologne 1983. For the 1980s and 1990s cf. G. Langenhorst, 'Die literarische Wiederentdeckungen Jesus in Romanen der 80er Jahre' and 'Jesus im modernen Roman. Schriftsteller auf den Spuren seiner Zeitgenossen', *Stimme der Zeit* 210, 1992, 751–60 and 819–30.

9. Cf. R. B. Saguier, 'Augusto Roa Bastos und die zeitgenossische Erzählkunst Paraguays', in *Lateinamerikanische Literatur*, ed. M. Strausfeld, Frankfurt am Main 1976, 167–83, esp. also 426f.

10. The original title of the novel was *Hijo de Hombre* (1959), revised 1982. The German appeared under the title *Menchensohn*, Frankfurt am Main 1994.

11. A. Roa Bastos, *Menschensohn* (n. 10), 362.

12. Cf. C. Aitmatov, *Karawane des Gewissens. Autobiographie, Literatur, Politik*, Zurich 1988.

13. C. Aitmatov, *Placha*, Moscow 1986; German *Der Richtplatz*, Zurich 1987, 244.

14. Ibid., 247.

15. Ibid., 299.

16. Ibid., 301.

17. Ibid., 226.

18. J. Saramago, *O Evangelho segundo Jesu Cristo*, Lisbon 1991; German *Das Evangelium nach Jesus Christus*, Hamburg 1993.

19. Ibid., 423.
20. Ibid., 437.
21. Ibid., 511.
22. This can only be hinted at in this context. It is substantiated in detail in K.-J. Kuschel, *Born Before All Time? The Dispute over Christ's Origin*, London and New York 1992.

The Difficult Jesus.
Problems of Discipleship

Norbert Mette

The sociologist F.-X. Kaufmann has sketched out the conditions of being or becoming a Christian in the context of 'radicalized modernity' (i.e. in the conditions of a constant acceleration of the process of modernization which tends to be limitless) in the following theses:

1. It is difficult to become a Christian in this modern culture.
2. It is difficult to live and act as a Christian on the premises of this culture.
3. For if one attempts to practise being a Christian, one causes difficulties for others.[1]

The spontaneous objection may be made to these theses that committing oneself to follow Jesus has always been a difficult matter. One need only recall Jesus' invitation to the rich young man who was unable to follow him (cf. Matt. 19.16–26). And the same thing has happened countless times in history since.

In fact, that following Jesus has its price has quite recently been re-emphasized in a very impressive way in the resolution 'Our Hope' passed by the united synod of the Diocese of the Federal Republic of Germany; in view of church life there as it is at present, the following 'signposts' to discipleship have deliberately been stressed:[2] the obedience of the cross, poverty, freedom and joy. Self-critically, the synod resolution warns that at best only something of all this can be discovered in the praxis of the church. The church resembles a 'religion of prosperity' rather than a 'religion of the cross'; a 'rich church' rather than a church in solidarity with the poor and weak; a church anxiously holding back from the risk of the freedom of the gospel rather than going on the offensive; and finally a church which tends to look anxiously inwards rather than radiating the joy of the redeemed.

In this text it is also generously conceded that not only are there external difficulties which put problems in the way of a consistent life of discipleship, but that there are also considerable reservations and considerable resistance within the church's own ranks – what Jesus already attacked as 'little faith'. Not least it was and is the form of the church(es) which results from this that prevents people from seeing discipleship of Jesus as a way of life in which it is rewarding to engage. Therefore the admonition of Pope Paul VI in *Evangelii nuntiandi* 15 that in principle the gospel is addressed first to the church remains very relevant.

However, in the following discussion the difficulties within the church which stand in the way of its becoming a credible community of disciples of Jesus and winning new followers for him will not stand in the foreground. The resolution of the synod clearly indicates that committing oneself to the discipleship at the same time means dissociating oneself from particular individual and collective patterns of behaviour (Mark 1.15, 'Repent!') and shows how this must be done. Without necessarily wanting to adopt the theological programme of the Christian community as a 'society of contrast',[3] one can hardly deny that Christian praxis brings one into open conflict with some of the predominant social practices and that precisely this presents a genuine difficulty (for both sides). The resolution 'Our Hope' expresses this by referring to Jesus' praxis as follows: 'Jesus was neither a fool nor a rebel; but evidently he could be confused with both. Finally he was mocked by Herod as a fool and handed over by his fellow countrmen to be crucified as a rebel. Anyone who follows him and is not afraid of the poverty entailed in obeying him; anyone who does not reject the cup, must expect to succumb to this misunderstanding and fall between all stools – time and again.'[4]

I shall be using Kaufmann's theses as a rough guideline in discussing the peculiar difficulties which arise for a practice of discipleship in our world, caught up as it is in a process of accelerated modernizing, especially in the societies of the northern hemisphere (though there is an unmistakable trend towards globalization). At the same time I shall indicate the problems which the proclamation of Jesus Christ, i.e. the explicit invitation to become his disciple, must deal with in such conditions.

I. What makes it (more) difficult to become a Christian

From a sociological perspective, becoming a Christian involves a process of socialization. Whereas in a society stamped by Christianity this was largely bound up with the process of socialization generally, clearly the situation has changed considerably as a result of the increasing gap which has opened up between society and the church. Even if in some places and at some times children are still socialized as Christians when they grow up, this is no longer the rule. For the majority of adolescents the process is quite the reverse: they are baptized as infants, but this fact becomes increasingly irrelevant to them. On the other hand, an increasing number of adults who have grown up with no relationship to the church are deciding to be baptized.

However, here more than external factors, which only give very limited information about the dispositions with which they are associated, are involved. The decisive question is therefore less what the situation is with the formal conditions of church recruitment, but rather how the conditions of socialization are created in the first place. Here I shall argue that several factors contribute to the massive difficulties not only in becoming a Christian but also in gaining personal identity, and that the number of these factors is increasing.[5]

In order not to paint a picture which is all gloom, I should explicitly point out that the slogans 'individualization' and 'pluralization' which keep being used to describe the conditions of socialization in (post)-modernity are by no means *a priori* to be evaluated in negative terms. Rather, the various spaces which have been opened up for individuals in the process of modernization are valuable and positive. Individuals no longer have to follow standardized patterns which allow of no exceptions, but can (and must) be shaped by their own assessments – a development which also favours the claiming of what Luther called 'the freedom of the Christian'. There are therefore good reasons for associating the beginning of this possibility with the Reformation.

However, there is no overlooking the fact that the increase in freedom in present circumstances which has come about in principle is being considerably limited, if not reversed. Quite a number of people feel that this relatively new situation, in which one need not and cannot follow a predetermined course, simply asks too much of them. They find it difficult to get their own bearings and to enter into commitments. Everything seems the same to them and therefore they become increasingly indifferent. Kaufmann writes that we get the impression,

that it is increasingly difficult for deeper commitments to develop, as though the processes of human maturing, which always also have religious components, are more difficult to go through successfully. So it seems as if not only the values of Christianity but also values generally are being internalized less. Identifications are becoming weaker and identities more superficial.[6]

It would be short-sighted to blame individuals here, especially those who have to grow up in situations which have become so difficult. For all those who market products – whether these are consumer goods or world-views – in their own interest have to present these products as the best, with the result that the 'customer' is confronted with the most varied promises and lures, some of which are even contradictory. Moreover, everything possible is done to influence customers subliminally so that they make certain choices. The rapid change of fashion and also the mobility which is demanded in the world of work and elsewhere adds to the impossibility of making long-term plans for living and acting. 'Live for the present' is the slogan which is propagated everywhere. And there are plenty of messiahs who promise immediate happiness: one only has to take what they offer – one after another.

In short, all this leads to a widespread mood in which people ask what someone who lived two thousand years ago, in quite a different time, may still have to offer the present situation, even if he said important things to the people of his time. Or this Jesus is pepped up so that he simply fits the present and meets its needs.

II. What makes it (more) difficult to live and act as a Christian

Even if we take into account the fact that becoming a Christian is a lifelong process that is never completed, it is expressed in particular forms of living and ways of acting. In connection with this the second thesis proposed by Kaufmann and taken over here claims that these forms and ways are difficult to realize on the premises of modern culture. This situation has already been partially described in the account of the present-day conditions of socialization. There is much to support the view that what is indicated there can be generalized, and that the rationality which has come to shape and direct modern society is based on principles which are diametrically opposed to the basic conceptions of Christian faith. Here I am not claiming that Christianity and modernity are fundamentally different. On the contrary, it is largely acknowledged that the Judaeo-Christian tradition has been a great influence in shaping some of the 'achievements' of modern society – above all in the sphere of ethics – and forms one of its foundations. However, in all soberness we must note that in business and politics – which have tendencies to colonize all spheres of life – maxims of thought and action have been proposed and established which are framed exclusively in terms of a rationality of means and ends. Where personal advantage or gain is envisaged and pursued without observing any limits, and where strategic action and the instrumental reason directing it become excessively powerful and penetrate the sphere of everyday communication, slowly but surely the resources for a healthy human society are undermined and consumed. There are plenty of signs of such a pernicious development. One might cite the extension of self-centred thinking in terms of careers, combined with a strongly hedonistic attitude; the increase of violence in society; the unadorned propagation and public acceptance of a neo-liberal ideology with strong elements of social Darwinism which serves to legitimate the thoughtless exclusion from society of increasingly numerous groups of people at home and even more in the international context. What can be a possible consequence of the process of individualization is increasingly becoming a reality: a break-up of solidarity which is assuming terrifying dimensions.

Wherever self-interest stands exclusively at the centre of the calculations and everything else is seen in the perspective of usefulness or furthering that self-interest, not only are the ethical foundations of a society shaken or eroded, but there is no longer any room for a religion which does not limit itself to a mere sacralization of given circumstances and a projection of the human striving for perfection. The logic and practice of the quest for increased power allows no religion which longs for a transcendence of the Wholly Other, in other words for something which human beings cannot achieve by themselves, but which is granted to them by grace and which finds corresponding expression in the unconditional recognition of all others and acts in solidarity with them. We may leave aside the question whether this 'crisis of God' has been aptly diagnosed, but the symptoms which J. B. Metz cites for it can hardly be denied. As he remarks in an interview,

We must ask ourselves the radical question whether there is something in our lives that is not at our disposal, that we do not want to be talked out of at any price. What we mean by the name of God is more seriously under discussion today than ever before. Up till now there has been something like a Christian civil religion in our society. Therefore the question of God did not affect anybody. But today we have long been living in a world which understands itself as a world after the death of God. The world is totally unmoved, totally untouched, not even atheistic in the classical sense. But this very indifference will not tolerate any religion.[7]

III. Why Christians are increasingly causing difficulties for others

In order not to give the impression once more that the Christian faith can be conjured up as a panacea for all possible crises and ills of contemporary society, I would like to preface this section with two remarks. First, a stocktaking of this society cannot ignore the fact that alongside the tendencies which are ultimately running towards self-destruction there are also notable counter-forces opposing these tendencies. For the most part this movement has not grown out of the Christian churches, and at best finds a place on their periphery. Nevertheless, quite a few of these initiatives and movements also point to the historical Jesus as a source and inspiration for their praxis. The second point is connected with this. What becoming and being a Christian involves is by no means a timeless matter, but has constantly to be rediscovered and tested in the face of changing circumstances. The more epoch-making the upheavals are, the more radical assurances are needed. To this degree the present situation of Christians and the churches can be regarded as a healthy opportunity. For it is becoming increasingly evident that there is no future for the kind of Christianity which has shaped the societies of Europe and America for centuries. What is more natural in such a situation than to reflect once again on one's genuine origin, namely the Jesus of Nazareth who is confessed as the Christ by his disciples?

It is not as simple to do this as those who go through the land proclaiming 'Jesus lives' and advocate a sectarian piety think. First of all, as I have indicated, for many of our contemporaries access to Jesus is blocked by the churches, which claim to have committed themselves to his cause.[8] Furthermore, nowadays as a rule he is concealed more than revealed by an abstract theological conceptuality which was helpful at a time when claims were being established about the significance of his person. But the difficulties do not cease even if one manages to penetrate to the original testimony of this Jesus. On the contrary, they begin precisely there. Here we meet someone who is far from fitting into our own time; in what he says and does he sharply opposes the message 'Blessed are the competent', which is propagated and followed everywhere nowadays. He takes sides with the oppressed and those in prison, and shows solidarity with the poor. He pays special attention to those who have been forced to the margin and excluded. He boldly breaks through the social tabus which have been given religious sanction. Even the 'holy' institutions of the temple and the market are not spared his prophetic criticism. It does not take much imagination to see why the ruling powers wanted to do away with this disturber of the social and (civil) religious order.

It is not surprising that this Jesus who stands on the side of the poor and the oppressed finds an echo among groups and movements who resist the self-destructive tendencies of today's society and stand up for alternative, more humane, forms of social life, and that they can appeal to him to support their concerns. But here, too, very often limits to the reception of this Jesus develop, particularly if his (social) ethical praxis is to be seen in the context in which it necessarily belonged as far as he was concerned: that of an unconditional trust that his own existence was indebted to and supported by the God whom he addresses as his 'Abba'. For his disciples, who had also been fascinated by Jesus and his praxis during his lifetime, the experience in faith that this God had shown unshakeable faithfulness to him beyond death was a reason for not breaking up in resignation after his crucifixion, but rather for banding together to tread in his footsteps and go forwards in the direction of the hopeful message of the dawn of the Kingdom of God.

This should be sufficient demonstration of how such a Jesus – and with him all those concerned with consistent discipleship – not only was difficult for his own time and soon caused scandal, but also has precisely the same effect on the culture of today. Anyone who shows such freedom as he did in inexorably enquiring behind dominant interests for the sake of the well-being of all and acts accordingly will at least be irritating, even today. Indeed, such a person will be irritating particularly today, especially if it is maintained that Jesus reveals the last claim of God in a way which is 'utterly inconspicuous and ordinary, human and historical'.[9] To raise such claims to truth and universality is generally regarded as crazy and outdated, at the latest in the context of the *de facto* popularity of religions, ideologies and world-views – though people tend to ignore the fact that the same claim is made for the technological and economic rationality which has largely broken through everywhere and is taken for granted.

IV. How can men and women today nevertheless be persuaded to become disciples?

It would be dishonest to give the impression that a generally valid answer can be given to this question – which understandably oppresses Christians.

This is not simply because at the latest, the individualization of plans and careers condemns to failure any attempt at generalization. In addition there is the familiar Christian insight that God has a single and unique history with each individual and that our knowledge of these ways of God is limited. So at this point where we are considering the question what could cause men and women today to become Christians, instead of making general statements, it would be natural to give a hearing to personal testimonies.

Though that is not possible here for reasons of space, this comment contains a first answer to the question which has been raised. People can hardly gain a relationship to Jesus if they are made to repeat orthodox formulations of faith which remain incomprehensible to them. They need to be invited and encouraged to trace the meaning that Jesus has (or does not have) for their lives and to discuss that. This is no cheap concession to individualization and thus a complete subjectification of faith. On the contrary, if the view that faith has to do with the possibility of human subjectivity is to go beyond mere words, this faith must also be capable of finding a place in people's lives and in the experiences which shape them. And where there is a personal exchange, it immediately becomes clear how Jesus, if he becomes existentially significant, inevitably takes on an unmistakable form and how there is a reciprocal enrichment here.'[10]

There are special forms of approaching and grappling with Jesus in art, whether in literature, painting or music. This rich and precious heritage does not just come from the past. Jesus is a special point of reference right down to present-day art, which constantly makes him its theme.[11]

Particularly in the realm of art it becomes clear that Jesus cannot be fettered with any institutional change. No only individually, but also collectively, there is a multiplicity of perceptions and receptions of his person. We might think, for example, of the significance attached to Jesus in other religions alongside Christianity.[12] Or also of the reception of Jesus quite outside the formal religions, as for example in movements for social emancipation. Many examples of this can be cited from the history of the workers' movement.[13] At present one might refer to the feminist movement, where Jesus is made a focal point and there is creative thought and argument about him.[14]

For all their differences, the ways of encountering and following Jesus here have one common characteristic: they do not necessarily stem from the significance attributed to him by Christian belief, though they do indicate that he is a person thought worthy of special attention. That this attitude can by no means be taken for granted follows from what has been said above. There is something to be said for thinking that the mere fact of turning to a person like Jesus and being concerned with him expresses an attitude which is not in conformity with prevailing conditions in so far as it requires a readiness to think it important for the present to remember the past, a longing for or a curiosity about the new or the unknown, a capacity to accept surprises and to wonder at them, a sensitivity to dimensions of reality which are deeper than the merely empirical, an openness to that which transcends the everyday, a striving for totality, a consciousness of the importance of others and a readiness for solidarity with them, a capacity for commitment and acceptance of the fact that one can go wrong or incur guilt, and so on. The decisive question is therefore where and how under present conditions those competences which seem to be basic to interpersonal relationships can be acquired and practised.

Here all that we can point to are spheres of life and experience in which those involved attempt to act accordingly and thus deliberately make themselves and others aware that they are not adopting the existing norms of society. Where this happens in the name of Jesus, where among his disciples there are the beginnings of a praxis of welcome and acceptance, of sharing and communicating, which is both spiritual and political, and instead of constantly feeling the need to achieve people are ready to accept freely,[15] the Jesus who inspires this praxis and his invitation to discipleship can exercise some fascination even on our contemporaries – and cause the offence that is necessary in this connection. That does not mean simply wanting to play down the difficulties mentioned above, but rather perceiving them all the more clearly. This is the basic presupposition for convincingly countering them with a praxis which is not just based on semi-reason. That it takes place under present conditions more on the periphery of society than at its centre is fully in keeping with the cause of Jesus.

Notes

1. F.-X. Kaufmann, 'Über die Schwierigkeiten des Christen in der modernen Kultur', in N. Klein et al. (eds.), *Biotope der Hoffnung*, Olten 1988, 121–31: 114f.

2. Cf. the resolution 'Unsere Hoffnung' in L. Bertsch et al. (eds.), *Gemeinsame Synode der Bistümer in der Bundesrepublik Deutschland*, Vol. 1, Freiburg 1976, 84–111: 103–7.

3. For criticism see N. Mette and M. Schäfers, 'Christliche Praxis in der Zivilgesellschaft', *Orientierung* 57, 1993, 135–9, esp. 136f.

4. Ibid., 104.

5. For the following in more detail see N. Mette, *Religionspädagogik*, Düsseldorf 1994, 13–42.

6. Ibid., 114f.

7. 'Wir müssen endlich anfangen, von Gott zu reden', KNA interview with J. B. Metz, 11 November 1995, 1f.

8. Cf. C. Duquoc, 'Jesus Christus, Mittelpunkt des Europas von morgen', in P. Hünermann (ed.), *Das neue Europa*, Freiburg im Breisgau 1993, 100–10, esp. 107ff.

9. M.-L. Gubler, 'Das faszinierende Ärgermis Jesus', *Diakonia* 22, 1991, 379–87: 386.

10. Cf. R. Englert, 'Stationen der Jesus-Begegnung', *Diakonia* 23, 1992, 37–43; S. Klein, 'Miteinander über Jesus Christus im Gespräch', *Diakonia* 23, 1995, 336–41. Cf. also the contributions to 'Forum: Wer ist Jesus für mich?', *Diakonia* 23, 1992, 5–13, and 'Forum: Wer ist Jesus für mich?', *Diakonia* 26, 1995, 331–6.

11. Cf. J. Imbach, 'Jesus – die geheime Bezugsgestalt. Ein Überblick über das Jesubild in der modernen Literaur', *Diakonia* 23, 1992, 54–58; R. Burrichter, 'Jesus in der modernen Kunst – eine Herausforderung für Theologie und Kirche', *Diakonia* 22, 1991, 400–2.

12. Cf. e.g. *ThuG* 86, 1996, 2: *Jesus im Spiegel verschiedener Weltreligionen*.

13. Cf. H. Rolfes, 'Marxistische Jesusdeutungen', in id. (ed.), *Marxismus – Christentum*, Mainz 1974, 34–58.

14. See the article by Cristina Grenholm in this issue, 25–34.

15. The 'virtues' listed here have their origin in base churches in France, cf. M. Gmelch, *Gott in Frankreich. Zur Glaubenspraxis basiskirchlicher Lebensgemeinschaften*, Würzburg 1988, esp. 148–68.

Jesus from a Feminist Perspective: Incarnation and the Experience of Pregnancy

Cristina Grenholm

Feminist perspectives[1]

Jesus can be viewed from a feminist perspective in several different ways. Feminism challenges traditional theological ideas about Jesus at several levels ranging from fundamental philosophical and methodological issues to questions about Jesus' relation to women and from epistemological discussions to liturgical praxis. Feminism cannot be reduced simply to one kind of activity or one single approach. There is a plurality of feminist perspectives on theology.

The starting point of the present article is that theological thinking about Jesus should take women's life experiences into account. Before that can be done we need to qualify what we mean both by *women's experiences* and *taking into account*.

In referring to women's experiences, we risk underestimating the variety covered by this phrase. We also risk projecting stereotype views of women. At this point I can only state that it is important to bear in mind the variety of women's experiences.[2] We should also pay attention to contextual significance, which affects both the experiences possible and how they are interpreted. In so doing, we reject every stereotype view of women.

However, we cannot dispense with the category of women's experiences. It is important to point out that women – as a group – have been neglected by theology, ignoring how individual women's experiences relate to each other. It is also wrong to overlook the fact that individual women's experiences are shared by other women. Affirming the shared experiences of women is one way of challenging the position adopted in cultures shaped by patriarchy. It helps us to go beyond the merely private sphere by drawing attention to the social dimension of women's lives. In doing so, we destabilize one of the important patriarchal dichotomies between the private and the political spheres.[3] By focusing on how many women share a particular kind of experience, we risk missing the essential point that women's experiences have a socially shared dimension. In my view, the concept of serial collectivity presented by Iris M. Young points in the right direction. It recognizes the similarities between different women's experiences without trying to universalize them.[4]

In this article I focus upon women's experience of pregnancy. The risk of playing into the hands of patriarchy is obvious. The experience of pregnancy is the basic ingredient in patriarchal definitions of what a true woman is and what she is not. Women's experience of pregnancy and giving birth is the source of the stereotype roles ascribed to us. This fact should make us hesitate before dealing with the subject. However, this experience is too important and too widely shared by women for it to be neglected by feminists in our theological reflection. There is also a need for a correction of our stereotype conceptions of pregnancies.

My proposal is that pregnancies (including miscarriages and childlessness) must be more adequately described. Feminist theologians often take the experience of mothering into account, as was done in this journal in 1989.[5] However, I have only seen vague indications referring to the complications of pregnancies. One example can be found in Elizabeth Johnson's *She Who Is*, where a more complicated picture can at least be read into her reference to these experiences as a basis for women's knowledge of the 'mystery of pain to life'.[6]

Why are the dark sides of pregnancies concealed in feminist theology? That is naturally a very difficult question to answer, but I can observe that in my country, at the far edge of northern Europe, miscarriages and childlessness constitute a widely shared experience. It is also one which society hides, thus fostering a false image of what pregnancy and childbearing is all about. In Sweden only a few books have been published which deal with miscarriages, and judging from the books available through the university library in Uppsala, the international situation would appear to be similar.[7]

I am aware that the main preoccupation of many – perhaps even of most – women is how to avoid pregnancies, how to preserve their reproductive health, thus overcoming the consequences of patriarchal oppression. We should also remember all those Third World women struggling to preserve the lives of their little ones. Still, I am not convinced that the grief of miscarriages and childlessness is only a pseudo-problem of privileged Swedish women. Even if it were so, it is nevertheless important for us and, I suspect, important for the form of patriarchy we are challenging, in the sense that the patriarchy look upon it as something to be silenced and kept within the private sphere.

What bearing should women's experiences have on theology? The role of experience in relation to revelation and tradition is of course a much discussed issue in theology. All I can do here is to clarify my position. I believe that women's experiences should be taken into account and that they should also have a corrective function in theological reflection. Since there is no knowledge of God which is not also shaped by human experience, all theology (including the theology presented in this article) must recognize that it stands in need of correction. In addition, I am convinced that it is essential for Christianity to include women's experiences, thus transforming both theology and church life and preventing the churches from becoming a curious relic from a distant past, incapable of responding to God's call to spread the gospel for the sake of the liberation of the world. Since women's experiences have not generally been related to Christian theology, they should have a critical bearing on theological reflection and boldly confront its androcentric bias.

Approaching Jesus

We can approach the topic of theological interpretation of Jesus in different ways. In this article I shall focus on the belief that Jesus is Immanuel, God with us. This is one way of expressing belief in the incarnation.

Most traditional christologies presuppose a Platonic-Aristotelian patriarchal ontology, further defined and labelled *kyriarchy* by Elizabeth Schüssler Fiorenza. The world is viewed as a hierarchy where God is placed at the very top and where human beings, animals and nature each have their respective positions in descending order.[8] The point of the doctrine of incarnation is that this absolute hierarchy has been overcome in the person of Jesus who was both God and man.

'Man' has often been understood as excluding female gender. Within the category of human beings, the male is ranked higher than the female. It is therefore quite legitimate, as Rosemary Radford Ruether has done, to ask the question 'Can a male saviour save women?'[9] In my opinion, she has quite convincingly shown that the effect of the patriarchal ontology is that salvation concerns only the upper part of the hierarchy, while women as well as nature tend to be (implicitly) excluded.[10]

Insisting that the belief in the incarnation should rather be expressed in terms of God's presence in the world through Jesus as Immanuel, God with us, is one way of immediately avoiding a kyriarchal hierarchy in our theological thinking. Approaching Jesus in this way, we aim at an inclusive interpretation of the belief in salvation. According to Elisabeth Schüssler Fiorenza, this accords well with one interpretation of the original Greek formulation of the Chalcedonian doctrine of incarnation, that of living among human beings.[11]

A more adequate description of pregnancies

God being with us, Immanuel, means that God has shared our conditions in the life of Jesus. According to Matthew and Luke, this includes his being born of a woman. What are the implications of this belief? That depends on how the process of being born of a woman is described.

Generally a pregnancy is understood as a process beginning with the conception and ending with the happy delivery of a child. However, this is not always the case. In Sweden no official records are kept of miscarriages. Their number has to be estimated. It is assumed that 10–20% of all *confirmed* pregnancies end in miscarriage. The percentage of unintentional childlessness is estimated at 15%. Within this category there are many women who endure a series of miscarriages.[12] The general view of pregnancy as something leading to a happy delivery has to be revised.

At this point there is yet another snare to be avoided in dealing with this topic, namely that of condemning intentionally interrupted pregnancies, i.e. abortions. This is by no means my intention. I think that we also need to have a nuanced view of abortions which has to be related to an awareness of their position within the context of a patriarchal society. This implies, for example, that while the responsibility for pregnancies usually is left to the woman alone, at the same time she is not accepted as a single mother.

There is an intimate relationship between the sorrow, agony, rage and pain connected with deliberately interrupted pregnancies and the sorrow, agony, rage and pain related to unintendedly interrupted pregnancies which needs to be further reflected on, although it cannot be done here.

Biblical support

The Bible is largely characterized by patriarchy. This fact can be viewed in various ways. One can hold that the Bible is impossible as a source for feminist theology, thus treating its patriarchal bias as something insuperable. According to this view, if the patriarchal traits of the Bible were to be deconstructed, nothing would remain. Consequently on this view feminist theology has to be post-Christian or pagan or something else.[13]

One can also cling to some form of historical relativism by holding that androcentric ideas are explicable from a historical point of view. It is possible to disregard them. A deconstruction of the patriarchal traits of the biblical texts does not reduce the biblical content to nothing. The problem of the androcentric bias can be overcome by biblical interpreters today.[14]

Although I side more with the pessimists in holding that androcentrism is a genuine problem in the biblical texts, I do not agree that a deconstruction of the patriarchal bias results in nothing being left. However, a necessary precondition for discovering in the biblical texts the liberating gospel which includes women is that they must be interpreted with the help of women's experiences as a critical corrective. Women's experiences of divinely condemned oppression and divinely given liberation must be taken into account. Elizabeth A. Johnson suggests working through the three steps of deconstructing, finding 'bits and pieces that hint at the untold stories of the contributions of women and the possibility of different construals of reality', and reconstructing theology.[15]

In this sense one could say that I do not look upon the gospel itself as sexist (or racist, or classist), although I also consider that it is imperfectly communicated in the Bible. Our experiences have an important corrective function. The underlying theme of liberation is almost always recognizable despite the disturbing noise of different kinds of oppression. You can hear the gospel just as you can hear someone playing Mozart with her window open when you are walking the streets of a city in the rush-hour. Therefore, to reflect on an image, a story or a theme which appears to have liberating power is not to deceive ourselves, but to place ourselves in a position where it is possible to confront sexism. I agree with James Barr that although the Bible is not perfect, it still suffices for theological reflection.[16]

Women's experiences are infrequently encountered in the biblical passages, but childlessness is a recurring theme. It plays an important role in biblical narrative. Elizabeth is one of the biblical women who reveal what is hidden in Swedish public life. So also does Mary, although traditional theology has prevented us from perceiving it. The two women are generally pictured as contrasting opposites, but there are also similarities worth exploring.

Incarnation and creation

How is it that creation theology regularly deals with the origin of the world with which nobody is personally acquainted, and hardly touches upon the creation of life in women's wombs, something personally familiar to the vast majority of human beings? The patriarchal interpretation of incarnation makes such a connection between creation and pregnancy difficult, since it consigns Mary's pregnancy to God's incarnation while at the same time assigning other pregnancies to the realm of fallen creation and sin. As Rosemary Radford Ruether puts it: 'Women, as representatives of sexual reproduction and motherhood, are the bearers of death, from which male spirit must flee to "light and life".'[17]

Understood in this way, the doctrine of the incarnation runs the risk of contradicting itself. The intimacy of God's interference with this world is by and large rejected and reformulated in terms of a cosmic process of the heavenly principle, the Word, visiting and transforming the world by means of a young woman who has more in common with a princess in a fairy-tale than with any other woman in this world.[18]

I have exaggerated somewhat in order to make my point clear. However, I hope to show that there is another way of understanding the relationship between creation and pregnancies which better expresses the meaning of the incarnation as God with us, Immanuel. This interpretation does not necessarily reject all other interpretations, but claims to add an important aspect by rejecting the idea of God's unique assistance in the conception of Jesus.

Mending the web

I shall now elaborate my view of the experiences of pregnancy, miscarriages and childlessness with which many women are familiar.

With the assistance of modern technology pregnancies can be confirmed at a very early stage. Readily available tests are able to establish pregnancy only two weeks after conception. A woman can be sure of the pregnancy and attentively register the symptoms. However, the symptoms do not originate in the foetus, but in the placenta which produces the hormones making her tired or sick. An early miscarriage often starts by the foetus ceasing to develop or even regressing. However, the placenta continues to produce hormones, providing the symptoms of a pregnancy. It is not until about two weeks later that the actual miscarriage takes place.[19]

The womb is a room for life and death. The life-and-death processes cannot be easily distinguished. The conception is a necessary but by no means sufficient prerequisite for new human life. Creation of life requires continuous support. Theologically speaking, it requires the continuous presence of God, giver of life. If God wants life to flourish, we must draw the conclusion that God does not always succeed.

Theological reflection which takes the sorrows connected with pregnancies into account cannot take refuge in a romantic conception of the wonder of creation. It also has to make room for the dark mysteries and unanswered questions of why all life that begins is not fulfilled. This is true of pregnancies, but it is also true of other parts of creation. In addition to growing seeds, many seeds never grow to be plants. Creation is never a total success; much which was intended for life apparently goes to waste.

Seen in this perspective life is always a victory over death. Life is always life which has been rescued and saved. Death belongs to the context of creation. There is a similarity between God's conquering death in the womb of Elizabeth and God's preserving life in Mary. A pattern can be recognized which applies to all human life, the pattern of death and resurrection.

In her book *God and the Rhetoric of Sexuality*, Phyllis Trible points out the connection between the Hebrew word for womb and the word for God's compassion.[20] If the firmament gives the impression of the power and might of God, the birth of a child could rather be associated with God's compassion.

Speaking of God as Spirit-Sophia, Elizabeth Johnson writes: 'The creative power that knits us into life continuously mends the torn fabric of our lives, forming in the process fine new and possibly surprising patterns.'[21] She also explicitly looks upon the Spirit as an instrument of renewal and empowerment in a context of brokenness and sin.

When seen from the perspective of pregnancy, creation needs to be expressed in terms of God's compassion and power to create life regardless of what has torn it apart. Of course this does not happen automatically. Life does not always conquer death. Life is always a miracle, depending on the assistance of the Spirit who is constantly involved in mending the torn web of human life.

Shared miracles

The biblical narrative concerning some of the major women and their pregnancies bears witness to divine assistance. It can be seen from the perspective of other women's miscarriages and (temporary) childlessness not as something exceptional, but as a paradigm which discloses the conditions of every new human being taking form inside a woman. It shows both its true context and its miraculous character in the sense that it is dependent on the assistance of God. Theologically speaking, every successful pregnancy is a witness to God's being with us, to Immanuel and the incarnation.

Christian tradition has prevented us from perceiving the parallels between our lives and those of the heroines of the Bible. The question needs to be asked: is it not the case that such a claim to affinity with Elizabeth's pregnancy as well as with Mary's reduces the meaning and importance of the incarnation?

In replying, we should also bear in mind the danger of reducing the importance and meaning of the incarnation if the similarities between Jesus' birth and the birth of other children is not acknowledged. This risk has in fact been insufficiently acknowledged, although docetism was judged to be heretical. God's incarnation in the person of Jesus implies his true humanity, that is to say, the connection between the living conditions of Jesus and ours. To endorse the connection between Mary's experience and other women's experience is one way on insisting on the doctrine of incarnation.

Furthermore, affirming the similarity involved in the divine assistance of pregnancies does not imply rejecting the unique character of the person of Jesus. A person is unique, although the process bringing that person into being is not. Furthermore, the miracle of life is not necessarily diminished by the number of times it occurs.

My point is thus not only that the doctrine of the incarnation can be affirmed without the acknowledgment of the natural process of pregnancies having to be denied. I also wish to underline that the importance and relevance of incarnation is more obvious if the similarities with Mary's pregnancy and other women's is emphasized. Furthermore, the intimate relation between incarnation and the belief in the resurrection, which is a prerequisite for Christian discipleship, is affirmed. Elizabeth Johnson expresses it aptly: 'As such, the cross is part of the larger mystery of pain-to-life, of that struggle for new creation evocative of the rhythm of pregnancy, delivery, and birth so familiar to women of all times.'[22]

According to Jane Shaber, Luke 1 can be read without presupposing divine fatherhood in a biological sense and by understanding the words of the angel as a promise of empowerment and protection. Such a reading accords with a reading of the Magnificat as praise of God's actions on behalf of marginal and exploited people. Mary shows the hope of a woman who suffered and has been vindicated.[23]

Referring to pregnancies as ambiguous processes, carrying the possibilities of life and death simultaneously, does not imply denying the doctrine of incarnation, but insists on its wide relevance. Neither does such an interpretation of the mystery of God's becoming human deny the paradigmatic and unique importance of Jesus, his message, life, death and resurrection.

Notes

1. The English text has been corrected by Dr Craig McKay, Uppsala.
2. See Elizabeth A. Johnson, *She Who Is: The Mystery of God in Feminist Theological Discourse*, New York [2] 1994, 10–12.
3. See Susan Moller Okin, *Justice, Gender, and the Family*, New York 1989, 14, 110–33.
4. See Iris M. Young, 'Gender and Seriality: Thinking About Women as a Social Collective', *Signs: Journal of Women in Culture and Society* 31, 1994, 714–34, 1–12. Cf. a critique in Anne-Louise Eriksson, *The Meaning of Gender in Theology: Problems and Possibilities*, Acta Universitatis Upsaliensis, Uppsala Women's Studies, A. Women in Religion 6, Uppsala 1995, 139–41.
5. Anne Carr and Elisabeth Schüssler Fiorenza (eds.), *Motherhood, Experience, Institution, Theology, Concilium* 206, 1989. See also Sallie McFague, *Models of God*, London 1987, 97–123.
6. Johnson, *She Who Is* (n. 2), 159.
7. Eva Sundgren, *Missfall: Kvinnors upplevelser, sjukvårdens roll och möjligheter* [*Miscarriages: Women's Experiences, the Role and Possibilities of Health Care*], Stockholm 1992, is the single monograph in Swedish on the subject since 1981.
8. Elisabeth Schüssler Fiorenza, *Jesus, Miriam's Child, Sophia's Prophet: Critical Issues in Feminist Theology*, London 1995, 12–18. See also Rosemary Radford Ruether *Sexism and God-Talk: Towards a Feminist Theology*, London [3] 1989, 72–82, 93–9.
9. Ruether, *Sexism and God-Talk* (n. 8), 116.
10. Ibid., 72–82. See also Johnson, *She Who Is* (n. 2), 161–7.
11. Schüssler Fiorenza, *Jesus. Miriam's Child* (n. 8), 20.
12. Sundgren, *Missfall* (n. 7), 11f.
13. See, for example, Daphne Hampson, *Theology and Feminism*, Signposts in Theology 5, Oxford 1990.
14. See, for example, Julie Hopkins, *Towards a Feminist Christology: Jesus of Nazareth, European Women and the Christological Crisis*, London 1995.
15. Johnson, *She Who Is* (n. 2), 29f.
16. James Barr, *The Bible in the Modern World*, London 1983, 118–120.
17. Ruether, *Sexism and God-Talk* (n. 8), 80.
18. See Schüssler Fiorenza, *Jesus. Miriam's Child* (n. 8), 185–7. Cf. Johnson, *She Who Is* (n. 2), 98f. for the cosmic tendency being fostered also by Sophia christology.
19. See, for example Ruth Bennett and Linda K. Brown (eds.), *Myle's Textbook for*

Midwives, Edinburgh, London, Madrid, Melbourne, New York, Tokyo [12] 1993.

20. Phyllis Trible, *God and the Rhetoric of Sexuality* Overtures to Biblical Theology 2, Philadelphia [4]1985, 31–4.

21. Johnson, *She Who Is* (n. 2), 138.

22. Ibid., 159.

23. Jane Shaber, 'Luke', in Carla Newsom and Sharon H. Ringe (eds.), *The Women's Bible Commentary*, London and Louisville, Kentucky 1992, 284f.

II · Jesus Christ – Icon or Idol?

The Quest for the Historical Jesus. Some Theological Reflections

Sean Freyne

The debate about the historical Jesus is no longer confined to academic journals or learned books. It is repeatedly the subject of articles in the popular press both in Europe and in North America, and television documentaries continue to be made about various aspects of the discussion. If Jesus is not always 'good news' for our modern secular society, he certainly seems to be newsworthy. We are a long way removed from the climate of 200 years ago when Herman Samuel Reimarus (1694–1768) could not publish his controversial views about Jesus. Only posthumously did they see the light of day, thanks to the Deist philosopher, Gotthold Lessing (1729–1781), who found them congenial to his own enterprise of presenting Christianity as an aesthetic religion based on the insights of a genius, but far removed from the various versions then on offer in the different Christian churches of eighteenth-century Europe. Today, it would seem, any and every opinion about Jesus can be expressed without public concern or *odium theologicum*. It is only those who challenge the sacredness of the Islamic foundation story who must be silenced. Hollywood has taken note.

The fact that this modern interest in Jesus occurs at a time when adherence to institutional Christianity is on the wane in the industrialized, Western world, is itself an interesting cultural phenomenon. It reminds us that the academic debates of the nineteenth century did not take place in a cultural vacuum either, as Albert Schweitzer's now classic *The Quest for the Historical Jesus* (1906) so graphically illustrates. The contemporary popular interest in the historical Jesus debate, especially in North America, is the direct result of a policy of cultivation by some (e.g. The Jesus Seminar there) of the communications highway which is part of our global culture. It is simply the popular front of what has been described as the third wave of historical Jesus research. In the view of one of its most notable practitioners, John Dominic Crossan, this wave differs from the previous efforts (the nineteenth-century liberal lives as a response to Lessing's and others' attacks on orthodox christology, and the existentialist phase associated with Rudolf Bultmann and his students in the 1950s and 1960s) in three important respects: it uses a *wider range of evidence*, drawing on extra-canonical materials, either recently discovered (e.g. Gospel of Thomas) or not properly evaluated previously (the sayings of Jesus in various patristic witnesses); it *integrates various approaches*, literary, historical and social-scientific, in dealing with the sources; its *philosophical presuppositions* are post-modern rather than romantic, liberal or existentialist, as in the case of previous efforts.

These are far-reaching claims. It is undoubtedly true that the data base from which Crossan operates is expanded considerably, but in the last analysis a negative judgment is passed on much of the evidence in terms of its historical reliability, especially the canonical Gospel material. On the other hand there has until recently been a reluctance to use the interesting archaeological data from twenty intensive years' work in Galilee in the discussion of relevant sources. A greater range of disciplines are today being employed in the study of the New Testament generally, notably the use of the social sciences, but as we shall see, their application is not always unproblematic. As to the third claim, namely the post-modern context for contemporary studies of Jesus, apart from stating the obvious, it is difficult to assess its precise significance, other than to suggest that researchers seem less constrained than was the case with both the liberal lives and the Bultmannian phase, by traditional theological claims about the definitive nature of Jesus' ministry for Christian faith. In the end it will be necessary to evaluate whether the current wave of historical-Jesus research has been any more successful in avoiding the pitfall of what George Tyrell at the end of the nineteenth century described as the reflections of liberal theologians' faces at the bottom of a very deep well. In order to attempt such a judgment, however, it will first be necessary to review some aspects of the nineteenth-century efforts and the salient theological questions that may still be with us.

I. The nineteenth-century quest in its cultural context

The eighteenth-century Enlightenment with its stress on the rationality and freedom of the human subject and the scientific revolution which sought the explanation of phenomena solely in terms of their natural causes inevitably posed a serious question-mark to the biblical stories in general and those relating to Jesus in particular. Reimarus and Lessing were Deists who denied any notion of divine revelation and posited the idea of a deity far removed from the affairs of humans. In subsequent centuries the critique of religion by Karl Marx and Sigmund Freud as either the 'opium of the proletariat' or a 'wish-fulfilment' further eroded confidence in the classical theological claims of the Christian churches, including those about their founder, Jesus of Nazareth. The Gospel stories about him had to be explained in ways other than simply reiterating their supernaturalist claims in an uncritical fashion. The nineteenth-century quest for the historical Jesus has to be understood against this background. The fact that it was largely conducted in the German academic world of liberal Protestantism gave it a very distinctive colouring, since many of its key practitioners were convinced that the Reformation had restored Christianity to its original simplicity. They thought of the kingdom of God as preached by Jesus in ethical rather than metaphysical terms, and saw the conditions for its realization within cultural Protestantism which espoused an ethical and communal form of Christianity, freed from the shackles of the dogmatic Christ of later Christian orthodoxy.

In an effort to reconstruct a plausible account of Jesus and his ministry, the question of the Gospels' veracity had of necessity to be dealt with, since rationalist criticism of their supernatural claims had discredited their reliability for many. The figure of David Friedrich Strauss (1808–1874) stands out in particular in this regard, since he sought to steer a middle ground between the narrow reductionism of the rationalists on the one hand and the naive literalism of the supernaturalists on the other, by categorizing the Gospels as mythical. By this designation Strauss was acknowledging that dimension of the Gospels which in principle is not open to historical enquiry, thus calling for a distinction to be drawn between different aspects of the narratives. However, with the prevailing view of history as 'things as they actually happened' and the search for objective sources which were nearest in time to those events, this acknowledgment of the mythical dimension of Christian narratives had to await the towering figure of Rudolf Bultmann in the present century before it could receive proper, if controversial, attention.

Strauss did not put the results of his own analysis of the Gospels to work in terms of a strictly historical reconstruction. His account of Jesus is, rather, deeply theological and heavily influenced by Hegel's philosophy of the world spirit. Jesus is a singular, though not exhaustive, embodiment of that spirit, since 'the finite can never exhaust the infinite'. Such an account did little to inspire more orthodox views, and Strauss eventually was removed from his teaching position in Tübingen. The quest for sources, however, continued unabated. Mark's Gospel was deemed the earliest and most untainted with its realistic narrative style, and another source was identified beneath the Gospels of Matthew and Luke, a collection of sayings of Jesus that was designated simply by the letter Q (German *Quelle* or source). Thus the two-source hypothesis, still very much in vogue today, was devised in the context of the debates about the historical Jesus. *Plus ça change . . .* , preoccupation with the earliest sources is still the concern of the 'third wave', except that now the tendency is to replace Mark and refine the Q hypothesis by the Gospel of Peter and the Gospel of Thomas, as in Crossan's work.

The liberal lives which Schweitzer exposed concentrated heavily on the ethical dimensions of Jesus' teaching, in line with the liberal ideals that their proponents espoused and that were believed to be embodied in the cultural Protestantism of the day. Jesus emerges as the teacher of a moral code that was 'the highest expression of the human spirit'. In the Sermon on the Mount and in the parables 'the inner power of truth immediately penetrating to the hearts of men' (*sic*) reveals itself in its world-historical significance. Thus Jesus' life and teaching formed a single whole that was the outer expression of the inner harmony he himself had achieved, leading to 'his complete openness to the world and perfect inwardness toward God'. One text from the Gospels, 'The kingdom of God is within you' (Luke 17,21), was regarded as expressing this unique relationship to God and to humans that was Jesus' self-consciousness, giving rise to his own gradual awareness of his messianic status and his disciples' acceptance of him as such. Unlike Strauss's Hegelian categories, the liberals had sought to safeguard the unique status of Jesus by entering into his inner life and acknowledging the truly universal dimensions of his ethical vision.

While liberal theology was still in its heyday, a new and very different emphasis was appearing in German biblical studies, namely, the History of Religions approach, which sought to emphasize the strange, the primitive and the unmodern in Jesus and in early Christianity. In contrast to the universalizing tendency of the liberals, this new approach was more historically grounded, by emphasizing the particularity of Jesus. 'Theology was forced by genuine history to begin to doubt the artificial history with which it had thought to give life to our Christianity', as Albert Schweitzer put it later. According to this view, when Jesus spoke of the kingdom of God, he was not speaking of human, ethical possibilities, but of a wholly other understanding of God's rule that was external and cosmic in its dimensions, in line with Jewish apocalyptic hopes. Johannes Weiss, in direct opposition to his father-in-law Albert Ritschl's liberal ideas about the ethical understanding of Jesus' kingdom language, was one of the earliest proponents of this view (1892). Schweitzer developed Weiss's notion further by suggesting that when Jesus' expectation of an imminent coming of the kingdom did not materialize, he changed his mind and felt the call to take on the messianic woes that were anticipated before the end, according to the Jewish literature. While Schweitzer is quite happy to rely on Mark's outline of the career of Jesus, others such as William Wrede went further in undermining this trust. Far from being a straightforward account of Jesus's life, Mark should be seen as a highly theological statement of early Christian apologetic in the light of the failure of the coming kingdom. However, it took the disasters of the First World War to shatter finally the liberal dream, and a new and very different voice was to emerge, namely that of Rudolf Bultmann, who would throw the whole project of the historical Jesus into question with his kerygmatic theology in an existentialist key. This is an issue we shall return to in the conclusion of this article.

The rapid survey of some of the more significant moments of the nineteenth-century quest was intended solely to highlight some key issues that might shed critical light on the contemporary developments. Despite Crossan's disavowal of the comparison, certain issues seem clear. The question of reliable sources may not have been as refined as it is today, but it nevertheless was a real concern emanating from the purist idea of history 'as it really was' which was the dominant view of the nineteenth century. Today we may be less positivistic, but the ultimate objective appears the same. Why else would the question of stratification of the evidence be so important to the Jesus Seminar? The liberal agenda, in line with its Reformation roots, may have sought to shed later christological formulations of the tradition, but it still attempted to safeguard the universal claims about Jesus in terms of his ethical teaching. In doing so it over-emphasized the contrast with his Jewish antecedents, thus feeding into and uncritically replicating the anti-Jewish biases of nineteenth-century German academic thinking generally. These questions, too, recur in the present situation, as does the issue of either an apocalyptic or an ethical Jesus. Before condemning the latest wave, however, in terms of the to us mistaken ideas of its antecedents, it is important to sketch the results of some of the more important findings of the present quest more adequately.

II. The 'third wave' of Jesus research

It would be tedious to attempt a complete survey of all the different Jesus types that modern scholarship has thrown up. As noted already, one major contrast with the nineteenth-century 'lives' is the different context for the discussion. North America now provides the setting, partly because the centre of gravity for biblical and theological studies has shifted from Europe over the last fifty years or so, but partly also, I suspect, because that North American society today has been aptly described as a nation with the soul of a church. In a way that is not dissimilar to liberal Protestant dreams in nineteenth-century Germany, one finds a tendency to identify Christianity with the American dream. The Jesus images emerging from such a culture will inevitably bear the marks of their origin, even if it would be misleading to suggest that that is the sole factor that is operative. I propose to sketch the picture in broad outlines only.

1. *A Jewish Jesus*

New Testament studies today, like all Christian theological discourse, take place in a post-Holocaust setting. Inevitably, therefore, the 'bringing home of Jesus to Judaism' which has been a feature of liberal Jewish approaches to Jesus is inevitably reflected in Christian scholarship also. The discovery of the Dead Sea Scrolls has fuelled the debate, sometimes also distorting it in so far as unwarranted, or even outlandish, claims are made about Jesus and the Qumran monks, whose library the scrolls presumably represent. The impetus that these discoveries have given to studies of the Second Temple period means that we are much more aware of the variety of Judaisms that were on offer in the first century CE, even in Palestine. Stereotypes such as *the* Messiah, as though all were agreed about the expected figure, or the legalism of the Pharisees, no longer have any place in responsible scholarship, and this poses a new challenge for scholars, anxious not to replicate the mistakes of the past by presenting a Jesus over against Judaism.

From the Jewish side the various writings of the Oxford scholar, Geza Vermes, have received most attention. In his view Jesus can be seen as a typical Galilean *hasid*, holy man or charismatic, whose life is the very embodiment of the Torah-true Jew, devoted to the ancestral religion and deeply trusting in God's care and protection. Endowed with God's spirit, he can be compared with various 'men of deeds' in the Jewish sources, whose prototype is Elijah, healer and doer of mighty deeds. The various titles for Jesus, such as son of God, son of man, even Lord, which occur in the Gospels can be understood as terms of address within Palestinian Aramaic without investing them with the later theological value that Hellenistic Christianity has attached to them.

This very eirenic picture is in stark contrast with that of E. P. Sanders, who concentrates on the deeds of Jesus, especially the incident in the temple, to paint a picture of Jesus as the prophet of an eminent Jewish restoration in accordance with prophetic hopes. Thus, Jesus' action in overthrowing the tables of the money-changers and his alleged threat to destroy the existing temple as a prelude to building a new one (Mark 11.15–19; 14.58) must be seen as part of a single vision for the restoration of Israel, based on various prophetic declarations. Other deeds of Jesus, such as the calling of the Twelve, the healing of the sick and confining his ministry to Israel, all point in the same direction. At the same time Sanders does not see Jesus breaking with his Jewish heritage in any radical way. The reported disputes with the Pharisees over legal matters for the most part stem from the later church and cannot be construed in a way that Jesus ignored the law, though in one respect he did differ from other contemporary teachers including John the Baptist, namely, the belief that God's kingdom was an open invitation to real sinners, irrespective of their conversion.

Vermes' and Sanders' work, for all their differences of approach and emphasis, are concerned with presenting Jesus very much within the Judaism of his own day, without breaking the mould. Other Christian scholars, too, though espousing similar interests, focus more on the conflictual aspects of his ministry *vis à vis* his contemporaries. Thus, Bruce Chilton sees him as giving personal experience priority over learned discussion in his use of the scriptures, and sees the incident in the temple as an attempt to restore sacrificial practice to what was originally intended in the Torah, not its abolition, as Sanders maintained. Marcus Borg sees Jesus as a spirit-filled holy man, focussing on the present rather than the future and challenging the purity laws and their political and social isolationism by eating meals with tax-collectors and sinners. John Riches is also concerned with the purity laws in his efforts to understand the innovative dimension of Jesus' ministry. He operated with a more sophisticated notion of language as a system of signs, which, though shared and conventional, takes on a personal dimension through use and association, thus enabling new and creative formulations of common ideas to be expressed. Jesus' kingdom language can thus be construed as innovative in terms of conventional understandings, thereby leading to the transformation of Judaism, to cite the title of his book.

2. A Cynic Jesus

Under this designation it is possible to group together a number of images of Jesus which see him as participating more fully in, and being influenced by, popular religious attitudes within Greco-Roman society than was the case among those scholars just discussed. While in general proponents of 'the Cynic Jesus' stress the non-Jewish dimension of the Jesus traditions, it is important to be aware of recent developments in our understanding of the interpenetration of Greco-Roman and Jewish culture for several centuries prior to Jesus. While the encounter was sometimes hostile, this was not always the case, and some Jews at least participated fully in the intellectual life of cities like Alexandria in Egypt. The specific question that needs to be discussed in this context is the degree to which such inculturation had occurred in Palestine itself, both in terms of its geographic spread and across social divisions within the Jewish temple community. The range of questions covers issues from language (Greek, Aramaic or bi-lingualism?) to economic and social factors, to religious practices and values. What also needs to be considered here is the bias of individual scholars, in so far as the Cynic Jesus image as well as that of a thoroughly Hellenized Galilee have a certain flawed pedigree from the past that does not always seem to be appreciated by some of their modern proponents. Thus, as Hans-Dieter Betz has shown, a revival of Cynicism as a world-philosophy, with Jesus as one of its outstanding examples in a deeply anti-Jewish and anti-Christian way, was espoused in the last century by no less a figure than Friedrich Nietzsche, while the notion of a Hellenized Galilee led one scholar during the Nazi period to declare that Jesus was not a Jew.

Despite such a cautionary note it is important to acknowledge that some aspects of Jesus and his followers' life-style – homelessness and the eschewing of honour and all worldly goods – do have similarities, externally at least, to what we know of the Cynics. But there are very real differences also, which can be overlooked when comparisons are being made. For example, Burton Mack wants to situate Jesus within a Galilee that is so thoroughly familiar with Cynic attitudes that when he speaks of the kingdom of God this would naturally be understood by his hearers in terms of the Cynic-Stoic idea that only the wise person is truly king, in this case meaning that the freedom which accrues from detachment from all human needs makes one really master of one's own destiny. F. G. Downing has made a very exhaustive study of ancient Cynicism, and he too is impressed by the parallels with the Jesus tradition, arguing that it is more probable that these elements go back to Jesus himself than that they were introduced later. According to him also, Cynic ideas would be perfectly at home in Galilee. At the same time, Downing is careful to acknowledge a Jewish element in the Jesus-tradition also, and notes one very important feature of Jesus' teaching absent from the Cynic sources, namely, an eschatological perspective.

The sub-title of Crossan's study speaks of a 'Mediterranean, Jewish Peasant'. All three designations are important to him in terms of his multi-faceted methodological approach, which in his view makes the present quest very different in character from the nineteenth-century one. For Crossan, Cynicism represented a popular mode of resistance to ruling-class exploitation in the Roman world, a form of non-violent counter-culture, whereby those who adopted the anti-social stance espoused by the Cynics in regard to dress, begging and general demeanour were able to ignore the otherwise harsh realities of the honour/shame ethos of the Mediterranean culture of the first century. Far from being introversionist, this vision had within it revolutionary seeds. By stressing the practical wisdom elements in the sayings of Jesus as authentic and relegating the apocalyptic as later accretions, Crossan is able to present Jesus with his band of followers as Cynic-like figures, not engaged in a mission of renewal to Israel but enacting their vision of 'a brokerless' kingdom of God in the context of 'embattled brokerage' that was Roman Palestine of the first century. This message is defined as 'open commensality', or a radical egalitarianism which proclaimed 'the immediate and unmediated presence of God to each and every individual and the concomitant unmediated presence of each individual to every other individual'. Jesus' death was the direct result of the atopical nature of his ministry of 'reciprocal exchange of meal and magic', combined with his saying against the temple, giving rise to his arrest and crucifixion on his one and only journey to Jerusalem. However, the accounts of his passion, death and resurrection in the Gospels are not based on any historical reminiscences, but are free, scripturally-based narratives serving the needs of the later church.

For all the unconventional nature of this historical construal, not least, in my view, its marginally Jewish and overly-Mediterranean quality, Crossan's work has a genuine theological concern. There will always be a tension between a historically-read Jesus and a theologically-read Christ, he writes, and this will be reflected in the dialectic between how we see Jesus then and how we see Christ now. But for him that tension and dialectic are creative, not distorting. There was no betrayal in the move from the historical Jesus to the Nicene formulation, in that Catholic Christianity from the start saw the historical Jesus as the manifestation of

God, irrespective of how this insight was formulated. By basing his picture of Jesus on the wisdom strand of the Q source rather than on some version of the Markan narrative, as has been customary, his christology appears more like a Jesuology, since its first proponents, namely the followers of Jesus in the Q community, were living and acting in continuity with his life to the point where faith and imitation were indistinguishable.

3. The social-revolutionary Jesus

Crossan's work could just as easily be seen under this heading, since for him the 'embattled brokerage' of first-century Palestinian society was the immediate context for Jesus' unique counter-cultural response. However, because he regards its inspiration as arising from the Cynic/wisdom rather than the apocalyptic world-view, it does not engage with the powers in the way that some other recent presentations of Jesus do. These particular treatments are indebted to the increased interest in the social-world approaches to the New Testament generally. In attempting to understand how social realities might have impacted on his public ministry, the Galilean social world of Jesus has become a matter of intense debate. How Hellenized was Galilee as a result of the circle of Greek cities? What was the nature of Galilean relations with Jerusalem? What were the internal social tensions? These and other questions are being canvassed, on the basis of both the literary and archaeological evidence. However, in so far as such discussions are theory-driven rather than engaged in more old-fashioned social description, there is a distinct danger that Jesus may be understood solely in terms of a social reformer rather than a religiously motivated prophet. Marxist class theory stresses socio-economic factors in social conflict, but it would be a serious mistake to reduce first-century Judaism in such a way that issues about purity, the temple and Torah observance were seen as mere ciphers for other 'real' causes at work in the society, no matter how intertwined various aspects of life were in pre-industrial societies.

Gerd Theissen, the Heidelberg New Testament scholar, has been one of the most influential figures in this approach, analysing the Jesus movement in terms of roles, factors and functions, in order to see how certain typical patterns within that society were replicated in this particular movement also. Jesus and his immediate followers are seen as wandering charismatics, supported by sympathizers within the local communities who have made virtue out of necessity by transforming certain social realities such as poverty and violence in a positive way, either by valuing them differently, as in the case of poverty, or by internalizing them, as in the case of violence and aggression. Thus, while the movement can be seen as emerging from the social anomie of the society, it nevertheless functioned in an integrative way in contrast to some other responses, such as that of the Fourth Philosophy, with its violent, anti-Roman stance. Richard A. Horsley, on the other hand, sees the Jesus movement in more conflictual terms as challenging the value-systems of the powerful elites by espousing the renewal of local community life, and thereby presenting an alternative vision to the predominant one, especially in terms of 'the spiral of violence' which he considers to have been the controlling factor. Elizabeth Schüssler Fiorenza applies a feminist critical hermeneutic towards an understanding of oppression in first-century Palestine by developing a model of historical reconstruction to make explicit the subjugation of women, both in terms of their being devalued within the Jewish religious experience and their exploitation in the Roman imperial one. In her gender-sensitive reconstruction Schüssler Fiorenza includes exploited males also and speaks of wo-man in order to underline the inclusive nature of Jesus' community as a discipleship of equals.

This categorization of recent Jesus books is very general, but hopefully it has helped to show the great variety of perspectives, methods and results within the current debate. Each has different strengths, but also significant weaknesses. Crossan's suggestion that the current quest differs from the first one in being thoroughly post-modern is certainly true to the extent that no one picture of Jesus seems to dominate the horizon in the way that a liberal Jesus did in the nineteenth century. One can also see the traces of twentieth-century concerns in other respects, such as the issue of the Jewish Jesus and also the influence of contemporary social and feminist concerns, whether implicitly or explicitly. Indeed there is a danger that Jesus himself might be vested in the post-modern garb. The focus on Jesus' words that one finds in some of the recent writing which emphasizes their enigmatic, subversive and indeterminate quality, especially his parables, is in danger of depriving him of any overall vision or intention. This danger has been well countered by James Breech, who points to the story-telling dimension of Jesus' parables in particular, which though not easily yielding the questions to which they are supposed to be answers, nevertheless still display an understanding of human existence which calls for co-existence with others as part of an ongoing story where death is not the ultimate answer to human life, irrespective of all appearances to the contrary.

Conclusion

Breech's response to some of the dangers of the recent concern with the sayings of Jesus in isolation from his deeds raises in an interesting manner the issue which the so-called new quest for the historical Jesus ably documented by James M. Robinson attempted to address in the 1950s. The 'new quest' was regarded as 'new' in relation to the nineteenth-century one already discussed, which finally collapsed with the death of liberalism in the wake of the catastrophe of the first world war. Thereafter, the towering figure of Rudolf Bultmann dominated New Testament studies with his radical existentialist interpretation of the kerygma and the denial in principle of the possibility of recovering the historical Jesus. In Bultmann's view the quest is impossible because of the nature of the sources, and Christian faith is a response to the proclaimed word without any need for the support of historical research. Eventually, however, the dangers of this radical scepticism for a genuine Christian faith were exposed by some of Bultmann's own pupils, and hence the new quest was launched, with its genuine theological as well as historical concerns. In a programmatic essay Käsemann wrote in 1953:

> The question of the historical Jesus, in its legitimate form, is the question of the continuity of the gospel within the discontinuity of the times and the variations of the kerygma . . . The gospel is tied to him who, before and after Easter, revealed himself to his own as Lord, by setting them before the God who is near to them, and thus translating them into the freedom and responsibility of faith . . . He (Jesus) cannot be classified according to the categories either of psychology or of the comparative study of religion, or finally of general history. If he can be placed at all it must be in terms of historical particularity. To this extent the problem of the historical Jesus is not our invention, but the riddle which he himself set us.

This statement was programmatic for the new quest, namely, the need to establish the historical links between the proclaimer and the proclaimed, over against Bultmann's scepticism about that possibility and his disclaimer about its theological necessity. There could be no return to the old quest, however, with its biographic interests, since the nature of the sources did not allow for this. Despite this legitimate difficulty with regard to the aims of the old quest, there were problems with the new quest also, in that Käsemann and others such as Günther Bornkamm were too narrowly focused on the kerygma of the death and resurrection and did not take sufficient account of the narratives about the earthly life of Jesus, as these too formed part of the kerygma about him. It is only with the advent of liberation theology and its stress on the accounts of Jesus' earthly life in terms of its engagement with oppressive structures that the transformative possibilities of these narratives for Christian faith today have been properly appreciated. By contrast, the Pauline kerygma of the cross/resurrection could more easily be transferred into an other-worldly domain that lacks a concern for issues of social justice now as part of Christian faith itself.

If with the hindsight of history the original quest for Jesus may be seen as naive and unself-critical, it is not clear to me that the third wave has succeeded in avoiding similar difficulties. Despite all the sophisticated discussion of sources and the casting of the net for relevant data more widely, one cannot avoid the suspicion that late twentieth-century concerns have been determinative both in the choice of relevant 'historical' evidence and in the resulting pictures of Jesus. Recently, Sandra Schneiders has called for a reformulation of the question by distinguishing between the *actual* Jesus and the *historical* Jesus. The former refers to Jesus' ontic reality, as a being who both once actually existed in this world but no longer does and can only therefore be evoked as memory, and now exists as the risen Lord and Saviour, accessible only through faith. The 'historical' Jesus is a literary construct based on the actual Jesus' earthly life, but not to be equated with it. Only that which is in principle open to public investigation can be regarded as historical, and there are many aspects of Jesus' existence, not least the claim to divine status, which cannot be investigated in this way. The Gospels are interested in the actual Jesus' earthly existence, but that is not all they are interested in, since in their authors' view that is not the only truth about Jesus. As such, they give us only a partial account of his earthly life, that which was considered necessary in order to mediate symbolically the actual Jesus both in his pastness and in his present, glorified reality.

This formulation of the task is at once more modest and more realistic, in that it means that the quest for Jesus is determined by the records about him, especially in so far as these have continued to shape Christian existence through history. Thus there are theological as much as historical grounds for giving the canonical Gospels priority over other ancient sources, which may well contain significant historical information. It is with similar presuppositions that I have also attempted to explore the Galilean dimension of Jesus' career. While the canonical Gospels' account of that aspect of his earthly existence can and should be scrutinized in terms of our burgeoning knowledge of the region from archaeological and other literary sources, in the end its theological significance must also be considered. This aspect has entered Christian theological discourse, not as nostalgic biography but as a statement of God's concern for human marginality and particularity. Our continued preoccupation with the historical Jesus is indeed justified if this aspect of the memory of Jesus is kept alive and active in our world.

Select Bibliography of Books Mentioned in the Text

Betz, H. D., 'Jesus and the Cynics: Survey and Analysis of an Hypothesis', *Journal of Religion* 74, 1994, 453–73.

Borg, M., *Conflict, Holiness and Politics in the Teachings of Jesus*, Lewiston and Lampeter 1984.

Bornkamm, G., *Jesus of Nazareth*, London 1960.

Breech, J., *Jesus and Post-Modernism*, Minneapolis 1989.

Bultmann, R., *Jesus and the Word*, New York 1934.

Carlson, J. and Ludwig, R., *Jesus and Faith. A Conversation on the Work of John Dominic Crossan*, Maryknoll, NY 1994.

Chilton, B., *A Galilean Rabbi and His Bible*, Wilmington and Collegeville 1984

——, *The Temple of Jesus*, Pennsylvania 1992.

Crossan, J.D., *The Historical Jesus. The Life of a Mediterranean Jewish Peasant*, Edinburgh 1991.

Downing, F. G., *Cynics and Christian Origins*, Edinburgh 1992.

Freyne, S., *Galilee, Jesus and the Gospels: Literary Approaches and Historical Investigations*, Dublin 1988.

Horsley, R. A., *Jesus and the Spiral of Violence. Popular Jewish Resistance in Roman Palestine*, San Francisco 1987.

——, *Sociology and the Jesus Movement*, New York 1989.

Käsemann E., *Essays on New Testament Themes*, London 1964, 15–47.

Lessing, G., *Lessing's Theological Writings*, ed. H. Chadwick, London 1957.

Mack, B., *A Myth of Innocence. Mark and Christian Origins*, Philadelphia 1988.

——, *The Lost Gospel. The Book of Q and Christian Origins*, San Francisco 1993.

Reimarus, H. S., *The Goal of Jesus and his Disciples*, Leiden 1970.

Riches, J., *Jesus and the Transformation of Judaism*, London 1980.

——, *A Century of New Testament Study*, Cambridge 1993.

Robinson, J. M., *A New Quest of the Historical Jesus*, London 1959.

Sanders, E. P., *Jesus and Judaism*, London 1985.

Schneiders, S., *The Revelatory Text*, New York 1994.

Schüssler Fiorenza, E., *Jesus, Miriam's Child, Sophia's Prophet*, New York and London 1994.

Schweitzer, A., *The Quest of the Historical Jesus*, London [3]1950.

Strauss, D. F., *The Life of Jesus Critically Examined*, reissued Philadelphia and London 1975.

Theissen, G., *The First Followers of Jesus*, London 1978.

Vermes, G., *The Religion of Jesus the Jew*, London 1993.

Weiss, J., *Jesus' Proclamation of the Kingdom of God*, reissued Philadelphia and London 1971.

Wrede, W., 'The Task and Methods of New Testament Theology', in R. Morgan (ed.), *The Nature of New Testament Theology*, London 1973, 68–116.

Jesus the Jew: His Interaction with the Judaism of His Day

John Riches

Over the last century or more, questions of Jesus' place within Judaism and Christianity have been fiercely debated. Was Jesus a devout Jew firmly located within the Jewish traditions he inherited *and* within the ongoing tradition of the Mishnah and the Talmudim? Or was Jesus the founder of Christianity, the figure to whose profoundly innovative religious intuitions Christianity owes its very soul and who is therefore the standard by which all the manifold expressions of Christian faith are to be judged? A consequence of answering this latter question in the affirmative has often been to assert (therefore?) that Jesus is to be sharply contrasted with his contemporary Judaism, which has then been caricatured and distorted.

Classic examples of this latter, Christian, approach can be found in Adolf von Harnack's book *What is Christianity?*, which gives a sketch of Jesus' religion starkly contrasted with the religion of his contemporaries: 'They [the Jewish leaders] thought of God as of a despot guarding the ceremonial observances in His household; he [Jesus] breathed in the presence of God. They saw Him only in His law, which they had converted into a labyrinth of dark defiles, blind alleys and secret passages; he saw and felt Him everywhere.'[1]

The counter by both Christian and Jewish scholars to this often blatantly apologetic emphasis on the distinctiveness of Jesus' usage has been to portray Jesus as someone who adopted *largely unchanged* the linguistic expressions and ideas of at least one contemporary form of Jewish thought. Johannes Weiss[2] argued that, like the writer of the *Assumption of Moses*, Jesus proclaimed that the expected triumph of God over Satan was at hand and that men and women needed only to repent and to await the coming glory. More recently, E. P. Sanders[3] has attempted to place Jesus within a particular category of contemporary Jewish thought, Jewish restoration eschatology, and has therefore stressed the continuities between Jesus' usage and that of his contemporaries. In a similar vein, Geza Vermes has argued for the close similarities between Jesus and Galilean 'men of deed' and proposed that Jesus should be seen as a 'charismatic healer-teacher-prophet'. Neither of these two latter scholars wishes to deny that there is a freshness to Jesus' use of language, but nevertheless they both present it as fundamentally in continuity with contemporary use and therefore locate him within a particular category of first-century Judaism.

One of the features of these debates which has led to confusion is the assumption that there is a direct correlation between Jesus' Jewishness or otherwise and the extent to which he took over and made his own Jewish beliefs and linguistic expressions of the time. But must there be a strict identity between Jesus' linguistic use and that of at least some of his contemporaries if he is to be seen as a faithful, devout Jew? Religious traditions are constantly undergoing change and development in their beliefs and therefore in the language which is used to give them expression.

Part of the problem here is, I think, that scholars have adopted a rather mechanistic model of explanation of the meaning of linguistic expressions. It has been assumed, that is to say, that if we are to understand an expression such as 'Kingdom of God' in the Gospels, then the best way to go about this is to look for some contemporary parallel which might provide the *source* of the Gospel use, where 'source' is understood as the cause of the linguistic expression being considered. This is certainly a much better strategy than say identifying the meaning of the expression with Immanuel Kant's doctrine of the Kingdom of Ends, but it has its problems. In the first place it assumes too readily that linguistic conventions do not change; second, it overlooks the fact that, even where linguistic conventions are relatively stable, particular uses of standard linguistic expressions may have interesting variations; and thirdly, it disregards an important part of the way we come to understand what someone is saying: which is by listening not only to a particular discrete utterance and decoding it in the light of our knowledge of the linguistic codes which he/she is using, but by listening to the other things that he/she says and observing the other things that he/she does.

Let me expand these points a little.

1. Communication within natural language-communities works on the basis of an agreement among speakers of the language to use words and sentences in a certain regular way. Specifically, what is agreed is that

certain sentences will be linked to certain other sentences *and* to certain expectations about what one might experience if the proposition expressed by the sentence is true. 'It is raining' is standardly linked in English to 'it is wet outside' and to expectations that if you go outside you will get wet yourself. That is to say that *sentences have the meaning that they do by being part of a network of sentences and expectations which is sustained by regularity of use within a given natural language community at a given time.*

2. However, even where people are using language in a fairly standard way we need to be aware that there is a difference between the standard conventional sense of a term and its use on any given occasion of utterance. If I say 'thank you very much' when someone spills my drink in the pub, that is clearly not a standard use of the term, though it is a use which is very clearly parasitic upon the conventional sense of the sentence. In effect the sarcastic tone of voice indicates that certain values are to be reversed.

2.1. Irony, humour and metaphorical uses are other common ways of stretching the semantic range of a given language. In metaphor we have the unusual conjunction of two terms with their networks of associations which, however, in some measure conflict or interact with each other. Characteristically, metaphors will *suggest* ways in which we may rethink and reshape some of our standard ideas as expressed in our standard linguistic usages and thus help us to see things anew.

2.2. Linguistic conventions may undergo more substantial modifications. Black Consciousness leaders like Steve Biko were forced to rework the associations of the term 'black' before they could use it within a programme of black consciousness-raising, deleting its negative associations, retaining certain links with colour, and adding to it other links: 'black is beautiful', *and* espousing patterns of behaviour very different from those expected of 'blacks' according to the prevailing conventions. Such reworkings may occur when our linguistic conventions prevent us from expressing what it is we want to say, as part of our search for new meanings.

3. It is an important corollary of a network view of language that we learn most about what a particular utterance of a sentence means by attending to the other sentences and expectations which the speaker links with it. This is not to deny that we need to know what language he or she is speaking and what the conventional links are within that language; it is to emphasize that the precise meaning and emphasis which he or she puts on it can be discovered only by tracing out *as far as possible* the sentence-to-sentence links and sentence-to-experience links which are made.

To return to our discussion of Jesus' location in first-century Judaism. I was suggesting that it is a problem with much historical scholarship that it has sought to explain the meaning of a given linguistic expression in terms of *its source* in other expressions; and that it has underestimated the extent to which major religious figures may modify the traditions which they inherit. We may escape the either/or of earlier scholarship by seeing Jesus as a figure who interacts creatively with a growing and developing religious tradition and do so, among other things, by creative use of language. There are, it seems to me, good *general* grounds for supposing that leading religious figures develop and modify the traditions which they inherit. Religions are, at their best, living traditions whereby men and women attempt to make sense of their lives under God and which they modify in the light of events and experiences which raise counter-expectations to those generated by traditional beliefs. What the account of linguistic convention and change which I have just offered does is to give us tools whereby we can *analyse* the ways in which religious figures *initiate linguistic and therefore conceptual change* within their own traditions. Let me take two examples, from first-century Judaism; two, lest it be thought that Jesus is the only religious figure who initiated linguistic and conceptual change.

First, there is good evidence that the early first-century figure Judas the Galilean was using kingship language in a relatively novel way when he proclaimed that God alone was king and urged Jews *therefore* to refuse to pay taxes to Caesar and to take up arms against the Romans.[4]

This is part of a surprising development in the Jewish tradition. Jews had borne foreign overlords 'relatively willingly from the time of the destruction of the Temple to the reign of Antiochus Epiphanes'.[5] How was it then that the belief that God alone is king could serve as a reason for resistance to Roman rule? For it is not at all obvious that this belief need either conflict with allegiance to earthly rulers in general or require violent resistance to the Romans.

In the first place there were tensions in Jewish thinking about the kingdom of God. On the one hand, God's rule was a present reality which was experienced above all in the Temple cult; on the other, it was seen as something imminent, but yet to be established. Judas' programme of conducting a holy war against the Romans was in effect an attempt to conform the present reality of Israel's position as an occupied power with the expectations of the imminent establishment of God's rule.

Secondly, Judas' understanding of the rule of God was prepared by changes in the understanding of God relating to changes in Jewish nomenclature for God. Names drawn from oriental court language, 'King of Kings', 'Lord', 'despot', 'dynast', when applied to God represented him as an oriental despot with absolute power.[6] Thus Judas' belief that God is sole leader and master is 'merely a final consequence of the . . . general Jewish view that God is the sovereign Ruler of the world and, in particular, is the Lord of Israel'.

Thirdly, as Jews began to affirm their belief in the absolute power of God in the language of the oriental courts, so too Romans began to clothe their earthly power in the language of divinity. Such claims to divinity as Octavian's assuming the title 'Augustus' (Sebastos) and Herod's renaming the town Samaria 'Sebaste' and erecting a temple for the emperor there will have incensed Jews and encouraged them to assert the sovereignty of their God in the political realm as well.

Of course in one sense Jews had always believed that God ruled over 'the political realm as well'; what was different now (and this is not brought out so clearly by Hengel) *was the way that Judas conceived the nature of that rule in the light of the shifts in understanding of God's kingship that had occurred within Judaism.* Whereas previously it may have been thought that God allowed foreign rulers to rule over Israel on sufferance, now it was thought necessary for God himself to exercise his power in the political realm. But of course this will have generated expectations, viz. that God would not tolerate the presence of usurpers in his land, which were by no means met in reality. Thus Judas' call for a holy war may be seen not only as an act of obedience to what he took to be a divine command. It was also an attempt to make the present turn out to be the way that would be expected if God's rule really were of the kind that he said it was. If you change the meaning of terms, you change the sentence-to-sentence links *and* the sentence-to-experience links, and if these then do not correspond to what is actually occurring, you may need to try to make it happen.

Secondly, Jesus' announcement of the Kingdom of God *at the same time as* he shared table fellowship with 'tax-collectors and sinners' strongly suggests that similar changes in linguistic conventions were being made by Jesus.[7] To be more specific, Jesus challenged contemporary expectations that when the Kingdom of God was established, God's enemies would be destroyed, and replaced them with expectations about his enemies being restored, forgiven and healed. This links, moreover, with his injunctions to love one's enemies and, I believe, with his dismissal of purity regulations which served to reinforce tight boundary control between the Jewish community and those outside. Here, it would appear, he is not only questioning the belief that God's rule would be established only when his enemies were destroyed or subjugated, but also prompting his contemporaries to think through the meaning of God's justice and mercy, notions which are of course central to the Judaeo-Christian tradition. The point, in relation to what I have said above, is that we need to tease out *as far as we can* the other things that Jesus said and did in order to discover what he meant by the expression Kingdom of God: it is not enough to look for close contemporary parallels or indeed possible sources for a non-violent use of the expression, though this *may* be helpful. More than that, we need to see how what else he said and did coheres and forms a network which gives his use of the language of kingship its intelligibility.

Further evidence for Jesus' attempt to deepen his understanding of God's justice and mercy and goodness is to be found in his often very sophisticated use of metaphor in the parables. The parable of the Labourers in the Vineyard in Matthew 20.1–16 starts with the formula 'The Kingdom of Heaven is like' and then proceeds to develop an elaborate fiction in which a number of different agreements are struck between the owner of the vineyard and the men waiting for hire in the market place. The dénouement of the story comes when the men are paid. The dilemma which the story poses lies in the fact that on the one hand the owner in each case quite *correctly* acts *within the terms of the agreement* which he has made with each particular group but that, on the other, what he does arouses resentment on the part of the first hired because they perceive it as conflicting with what is just.

The owner's words at the end of the story serve only to underscore the dilemma. He insists that he has not wronged the first hired. The fact that he paid more pro rata to the last hired was his own choice and he was acting within his rights to do so. The verb *exesti* ('Am I not allowed, is it not lawful for me, am I not free to do what I choose with what belongs to me?') here might well be thought to have a more strictly legal sense in view of its predominantly legal use in Matthew,[8] but it is a term with a wider use, and this is reflected in the remainder of the owner's speech, where the focus is on the goodness or otherwise of his *will*. He attempts, that is, to shift the debate from the *legal* terminology about agreements, rewards, what is right and just, which has dominated the main part of the story to the *moral*, what is evil, good, via the bridge of this more elastic term (what is lawful, permitted, possible).

Now this move from the legal to the moral is also prepared at one point of the earlier narrative: what distinguishes the last hired from all the others is that they are simply sent into the vinyeard, without any agreement or indication of what their wages will be. They are at the mercy of the owner precisely because of their economic powerlessness: they have no rights or claims on the man. Towards the end of the day they have no option but to take whatever they can get.

All this is a complex metaphor which makes us think about the nature of human justice and agreements and then prompts us to think further about the nature of *divine* justice and mercy. So what is being said? Is it, as Bornkamm suggested, that 'God's mercy knows no bounds'?[9] That God's rule is not bounded or informed by notions of justice and agreement but rather by abject powerlessness on the side of the human beings and boundless unmerited mercy on the side of God? Clearly not. The whole point of the story is not to *dismiss* notions of agreements and rewards: the last hired are in an *anomalous* situation, one, that is to say, where the market forces ('no one hired us') have left them without any bargaining power and consequently with no means of supporting themselves. There is certainly no explicit suggestion that I can see that the whole market mechanism of agreements and payments needs to be replaced: rather a question about what it is right/good to do when it fails a group of people through no fault of their own. And yet of course the point of the story is that there does come a time when such mechanisms lead to a dilemma from which there seems to be no way out and which therefore invites the reader to a more radical rethinking of the relationship of market forces, civil law, natural justice and morality. For what is shown is that notions of natural justice (what is fair, what is right) do on occasion conflict with the proper functioning of the market place, the civil order; *and* that such notions of natural justice may also conflict with wider notions of morality: what is good, how one should conduct oneself in situations where the rule of law has broken down or where civil agreements and processes end up by destroying or victimizing some. That is to say, the networks of associations of these terms overlap and conflict: bringing them together in a story like this prompts the listeners to go away and rethink these associations in relation both to the realm of human economic activity and to the realm of God's dealings with his people.

So, again, what is the bearing of this on the understanding of the notion of the kingdom of *God*? *Not* that therefore God's dealings with his people are no longer to be conceived in legal categories at all. The point is rather that the relationship of legal categories to notions of God's justice and goodness and unmerited generosity needs to be rethought. Moreover, and this is the function of metaphor: there is no simple and unqualified direction given as to how this is to be done. Part of the task will be for those who hear the story to allow it to interact with their own experience and thereby to suggest ways of enlarging their understanding of God's dealings with his people. What we may glimpse in Jesus' parable is the interaction with the experience of those who found themselves marginalized within their own society, with its complex system of religious priestly rule and foreign overlordship, 'the last'. How would such a parable speak to the 'tax-collectors and sinners' of Jesus' day who were categorized as having broken faith with the religious norms of the Jewish community? May the point of the story to them have lain partly in the designation of the last hired as 'not working', with its association of not doing works of the Law (rather than as 'lawless'; cf. the designation of sinners as the sick in Mark 2.17) and partly in the invitation to *go* into the vineyard, which carries with it the promise of both work and reward? And is the point of the dénouement that such an invitation to those who are outside the community does not break with God's covenants with his people, the 'first-hired'; does not undermine the basis of law, but roots the covenants and the Law more deeply in the generosity and goodness of God?

To conclude. The question whether Jesus was a devout Jew may sometimes be taken as a question whether he simply adopted the forms of expression and thought of his day. But faithfulness to a religious tradition is not simply a matter of conservation of inherited forms. In so far as a religion is a living tradition which enables men and women to make sense of their experience under God, it is one which enables them to continue their search for the truth, in the light of changed circumstance and fresh insight or modification of ideas. Jesus is by no means unique in having contributed to the development of his religious tradition. The question which his freshness and originality poses for both Jews *and Christians*, who wish to claim him for themselves, is how far they are willing to listen to the profound and often disturbing questions which he has to put, how far in other words they have – and have had – ears to hear.

Notes

1. A. von Harnack, *What is Christianity?* (1900), reissued New York 1956, 50.

2. Johannes Weiss, *Jesus' Proclamation of the Kingdom of God* (1892), reissued Philadelphia 1971.

3. E. P. Sanders, *Jesus and Judaism*, London and Philadelphia 1985.

4. The key texts are *Jewish War* 2, 118: Judas 'incited his countrymen to revolt, upbraiding them as cowards for consenting to pay tribute to the Romans and tolerating

mortal masters after having God for their Lord'; and *Antiquities* 18, 23, where we are told that the fourth philosophy is like the Pharisees in all respects 'except that they have a passion for liberty that is almost unconquerable, since they are convinced that God alone is their leader and master'.

5. See Martin Hengel, *Die Zeloten. Untersuchungen zur jüdischen Freiheits-bewegung in der Zeit von Herodes I bis 70 N.Chr.*, Leiden 1961, 94, 102. English translation *The Zealots, An Investigation into the Jewish Freedom Movement in the Period from Herod I until 70 AD*, Edinburgh 1989.

6. Cf. e.g. Judith 9.12; GenApoc 20.12f.; III Macc.2.2.

7. See my *Jesus and the Transformation of Judaism*, London 1980.

8. 12.1, 10,12 in relation to the Sabbath; 14.4 in relation to the unlawfulness of Herod's relationship to Herodias; 19.3 in relation to grounds of divorce.

9. G. Bornkamm, 'Der Lohngedanke im Neuen Testament', in *Studien zu Antike und Christentum*, Munich 1970, 69–92: 82. The owner's decision 'breaks through all boundaries of civil order and justice. No scales of remuneration could ever be set up on these principles. Thus the notion of rewards which was so carefully worked into the narrative is rejected because precisely by contrast with all human concepts of reward and achievement, of justice and fairness, God's sovereignty is to be demonstrated by his goodness (Matt. 20.15). This then is the meaning of God's kingdom (20.1): *God's mercy knows no bounds*.'

The Christology of the Primitive Church: The Cost of a Cultural Mediation

Joseph Moingt

At the beginning of christology there is a semantic change, marked by the addition of the term 'logos' to the name Christ. This is a cultural change from biblical thought towards Hellenistic thought, as a result of which (at a price) Christian faith has come to think of itself and express itself in a rational type of language, as a science (an '-ology'). That might seem a banal comment, but then the assessments need to be made, and they can be and are extremely varied. Some praise emergent Christianity for so quickly appropriating the most prestigious and universal culture of the time, while others reproach it for having departed from biblical authenticity so soon. A similar question is raised about Philo: did he remain a 'Jew' or become a 'Greek'? The reconciliation which is often attempted – he was a Jewish believer who thought in Greek – is too like an evasion really to give satisfaction, despite its grain of truth, and the discussion keeps beginning all over again. I, too, am afraid of being dragged into a discussion from which there is no way out. The question which I have been asked to consider – and I have used it literally in the title of this article – is to evaluate 'the cost of the cultural mediation' which produced the christology of the first Christian centuries. I shall try to get as close as I can to the heart of the problem, which is eminently theological and epistemological rather than historical, and suggest an approach which is not too partisan.

I shall begin by challenging the fact that I have just stated as self-evident, namely the reality of a cultural shift at the beginnings of Christianity. The Christians of the first centuries only ever knew a biblical corpus in Greek, whether this was the language of the first versions of the

Gospels or the linguistic knowledge of some writers of this period. From the end of the apostolic age, because the Jewish communities were closed to Christian propaganda, Christian communities developed almost solely in the areas in which the majority of people spoke Greek or Latin, and Christians had only one of these two languages, especially Greek, either to address the people to whom they wanted to proclaim the gospel or to discuss Christian doctrine among themselves. So they were never led astray from a first and basic *veritas Hebraica*, to use Jerome's expression, to the process of 'Hellenization' which in our day is readily attributed to the early Christian theologians. The Christian *truth* could not be evaluated in linguistic terms, and there is little point in pretending that we can get closer to it by returning to the Hebrew or Aramaic presupposed under the Greek of our Gospels to reinterpret them in the light of the ancient scriptures, themselves also re-read in Hebrew. This truth can only be more important with reference to the *regula fidei* attested at the heart of the New Testament by the preaching of the church. It is in this area that we must examine what 'cultural mediation' can have been exercised, and at what 'cost'.

Now it is right to note that the first theological expressions that the Christian faith was to receive outside the canonical writings departed from the system of symbolic references to the biblical corpus from which they drew their meaning as affirmations of faith, taking on a different meaning in relation to another symbolic order which was used as a means of communication in another cultural sphere. I deliberately say a 'different' sense, rather than one that is alien or opposed, since the biblical references were always to exert a basic control on theological reflection. But other cultural references were to modify the sense of the first ones by adding to them and thus 'translating' them into a world of thought which was no longer that of the biblical authors, and into a language which 'thought' and conceptualized, and was no longer that of the Gospel narratives. We shall follow the first step in this development, paying attention to the further developments which it presages.

The first concept to demonstrate the express intention to go beyond the limits of the Gospel narrative in order to affirm faith in Christ is that of the 'pre-existence' of Christ which appears, roughly speaking, in the middle of the second century. In his *Dialogue with Trypho*, ch. 38, Justin distinguishes between two kinds of 'demonstration' of faith: one is content to establish that Jesus is 'Christ'; Justin observes that a number of Jews acknowledge this who look only for a human Christ, 'born man among men'. The other goes much further and thinks to prove that 'this Christ, being God, pre-exists the centuries and then, having become man, deigns to be born, and that he is therefore not at all a man among men', 'that he has pre-existed, being son of the creator of the universe, being God, and that he was born man by the virgin'. The change in language compared with the writings of the New Testament is not the emphasis put on the divine sonship of Jesus or even on his divinity, but the inversion of the meaning of the Gospel narratives produced by this notion of pre-existence. Even if it was inspired by some passages of the apostolic writings (but not literally, and these origins are not cited), or seemed implied (more probably) by the accounts of the virgin birth, this idea diverts the believer's view of the Easter event, which sees Jesus established as Son of God in the glory of the Father, according to Paul's teaching, towards his appearance on earth, and even earlier, towards his origin at the beginning of time. Despite the support that it can find there, theology can provide this demonstration only by departing from the historical framework of the Gospels: the account of the ministry of Jesus is succeeded by a discourse about origins.

This is not – yet – an evasion of history, since the argument consists in reciting the stories of the patriarchs and the prophets and showing that it was the Son of God who appeared to the former and spoke to the latter, but it is a different story from that of Jesus, or at least it is his 'prehistory' as Christ, to the degree that his pre-existence counts from but before his human birth. Unlike the messianic argument, which already sought to prove in the speeches of the apostles that the prophecies of the Old Testament applied to Jesus and that they were realized in him, this discourse, which is strictly 'theological' because it relates to the divinity of Jesus, undertakes to recount the presence and activity of the son of God on earth before his incarnation, according to which he 'is called to be a messenger and envoy, because he proclaims what has to be known and he is sent to reveal all that is proclaimed' (*Apology* 63,5).

So this discourse has not cut links with the narrative, but is in process of doing so to the degree that it cannot achieve its demonstration without going back even before the beginning of the history and taking its stand there to affirm that Christ derives his origin from God. Another word, 'Logos,'[1] makes it possible to cross this threshold.

How did this word enter into Christian discourse? This is a subject which is keenly discussed. Many theologians argue that it could only come from the Prologue of John even if it also derived from other sources, and could have no other sense than its biblical sense of Word of God, even if this sense was mixed with other, philosophical, meanings.[2] The concessions with which these professions of faith believe they have to surround themselves do not tell in favour of this view. It seems to me permissible to evaluate the cultural mediation played by the term Logos without entering into the kind of learned debate which would not be in place here.

In fact, rather than supposing that the first theologians to use this term did so under the authority of the Johannine Prologue, which has not been demonstrated, it would seem evident that people shaped in Hellenistic culture who were orators by profession before being converted to Christianity, as was the case with the Apologists of the second century, would spontaneously have used the term as they had done so previously in the well-known sense given to it by the culture of the time. And it would seem no less evident that the redactor of the Johannine Prologue, whatever biblical reference he may have had in mind, could not have ignored the cultural significance of this name, the significance given to it at the same time by Alexandrian Judaism in its commentaries on the Old Testament. Philo is the most distinguished example of this.[3] So only strong dogmatic prejudices can prevent the recognition that the presence of the word Logos in Christian doctrine is the operative factor and the indication of a cultural shift of prime importance in relation to the symbolism of the Old Testament, which is still very much alive in the New.

The Logos is no longer the effective word of God which commands and does what it says; it is the thought by which God conceives all things in himself and then puts them in order in the world: Justin explains that the demons, 'knowing that God had made the world after having conceived it by the Logos, called this first conception Athene' (*Apology* 64.5). The word Logos has the same meanings and functions in the discourse of the theologians as in that of the Stoic philosophers: the order of the world, the moral order, rationality, the quest for truth, all that being the reflection of the divine thought. The images of the mental word engendered by thought, of inner discourse and discourse expressed outwardly, which are used by the Apologists to explain the generation of the Logos, are another illustration of the Hellenistic provenance of this concept.[4] Other references, this time to mythology, move in the same direction. I have cited the allusion to Athene; here is another: 'Regard this Son of God called Jesus . . . when we say that he was engendered from God, in a different way from the ordinary mode of birth, as being equivalent to what you say of Hermes as Logos and messenger of Zeus' (*Apology* 22.1–2). For Justin, mythology tells lies in what it relates of the sons of God, who have never existed, but not completely, since several of these accounts have been verified in the case of Christ: so it offers a reservoir of figures and statements which confirm those of the Bible and accredit the appearances of the Word in history before his birth, though in a symbolic register which is evidently quite different. Finally, this name of Logos did the valuable service of explaining that Jesus was not Son of God in the same manner as the sons of Zeus (ibid., 21), and did away with the mockery, prompted by the announcement of a new son of God, among educated people who were getting rid of the old mythologies.[5] At the same time it drew the name 'son' into a semantic field which was no longer that of its application to Christ in the New Testament.

In effect, when Jesus calls himself or is called by the biblical name of Son of God, this name is interpreted by being set in a history of salvation which links God with human beings by a personal and singular relationship that unites him to the one whom he sends on mission among them: we remain at the historical level. But the comparison of Christ with the mythological sons of god which was inevitable in a world that was still pagan led to his relationship to God being set within a framework of divine genealogies and natural generations, and thus escaping the world and history. The name Logos was given to the same attributes by virtue of its assimilation to the name Son. Gnostic theology launched itself into abundant speculations about the divine generations or emissions or prolations; this produced a new mythology, this time crystallized around the Christian name of Son or Word, resulting from the projection of this name on to the Hellenistic heaven of divine beings to the point where it replaced the biblical history of salvation with a new purely celestial soteriology.

Irenaeus saw the danger and wanted to prohibit theologians from speculating on this 'generation which cannot be narrated', but these theologians were prevented by other heresies from taking refuge in silence. When Christians at the beginning of the third century, frightened at the idea of talking of the Father and the Son as though they were two Gods, wanted to combine them as one God on the pretext that the name Logos – translated by Word – did not denote anything of substance, but only a sound, it proved necessary to explain – to give narrative form to? – this 'generation which cannot be narrated'. That is what Tertullian did: taking up the image of the word in the mind, he explained that the divine reason, thinking of the world, produced within itself an inner discourse, necessarily subsisting because it is the very substance of God, namely the Logos which it engendered by making it emerge to create the world.[6] This was not far from the concept of immanent and eternal generation which the Council of Nicaea was to canonize a generation later. Theology had made unquestionable speculative progress, but for a long time it was distracted from the 'stories' of salvation towards a fixation on the contemplation of the 'heavenly' mysteries.

I must interrupt this historical analysis, brief though it has been, which has placed the christology of the primitive church in the cultural setting that it created for itself, to develop my reflections on the 'cost' of this 'cultural mediation'. We often tend to put the greatest weight on the dogmatic statements which were not to appear until the fourth and fifth centuries, i.e. long after the period at which I stopped my analysis, statements whose conceptual language in fact clashes brutally with that of the Gospels. But at that time these statements were only providing replies to the questions which were inevitably raised the moment the interest of faith came to be fixed on the form of the divine origin of Christ, and which had no less inevitable repercussions on the way in which the Son of God became man. So the decisive cultural shift comes earlier; it takes place at the point when and to the degree which the ground is chosen on which emergent Christianity organizes its propaganda, namely the mythical ground of a generation 'which cannot be narrated' since what happens before any beginning no longer belongs within the narrative order. The question of the origin of Christ is certainly raised by the gospel itself, but it calls for an answer in the same terms in which the question is raised, in the concrete terms of a history of salvation which can be told because it takes place between God and humanity, on our earth and in our time. As soon as it leaves the situation of the question, its points of reference and its limits, the quest for an answer takes the course of myth. Having made this statement about a precocious cultural 'derivation' of Christian theology, I would like to add that I do not think that it fails to be loyal to the faith – far from it. I even think that it is inevitable and necessary, and finally fruitful to use it as a starting point.

The faith of second-century Christians in the 'pre-existence' of Christ as Son of God was clearly based on his resurrection, in conformity to the teaching of the New Testament; but equally, and perhaps by preference, it was based on the message and account of the virginal conception and also on the Old Testament narrative, which seemed to present the appearances of a divine messenger, appearances which were taken literally without being deciphered. Moreover, quite naturally, it was based on the very usage of the name Son of God which was not understood differently when read in the Gospels from the way in which it was used in connection with the sons of the gods of Olympus; it was understood with infinitely more respect, but in the same order of meaning, as a religious belief of mixed provenance which even occurred in the Bible. It lent itself to the welcome of the Christian faith and spontaneously drew that faith towards the sphere of mythical representations. It was not pagan belief which served to divinize Christ, as some historians argued in the last century, since his divinity, understood as the bond which unites him to God in the same 'economy' of salvation, is the basic preunderstanding of Christian faith. However, Christian faith, while drawing its arguments from the sacred scriptures and not from elsewhere, took its signifiers from the Hellenistic religion and the culture which had shaped the minds of these believers. Once again, if we are allowed to criticize them, it is not for having borrowed from the culture of the time – what else do we do? – but for having allowed themselves to be distracted from all that for us today constitutes the history of Jesus Christ, revelation and salvation: that is the real 'cost' of this move.

But could things have been otherwise? Can we imagine that it would have been possible to proclaim Jesus Son of God in a world full of engendered deities without allowing comparison with them? And this confrontation could only take place by accepting the mediation of the same cultural and religious language. The Christians of the time were able to set the historical truth of the biblical accounts against the 'lies' of the pagan myths. But they did not have the same idea of history as we do, and sought in these narratives above all the 'revelation' of hidden 'mysteries', with the same prejudices as their pagan contemporaries had towards other texts which were equally regarded as sacred. The fatal cost of this approach in terms of mystery was a removal from the realities of history.

This cultural mediation was inevitable; even more, it was necessary for the very proclamation of the faith. I am not speaking here of the needs of linguistic communication, which are always inevitable, but those of cultural communion, which relate to the knowledge of the other and its truth. The use of a language can be reduced to utilitarian contacts without depth; the acceptance of a foreign culture is a gesture of displacement, of understanding, of acquiescence in its values, of appropriation, of an exchange which does not take place without a relative alteration to each person's original culture. Anyone who wants to pass on a message to someone else must fall in with the criteria of credibility and verification which condition its reception by the other. This law of communication is particularly important for the gospel faith as it moves from Israel to the nations, resisting being enclosed in a sacred precinct and becoming open to others in so far as it is not established under a law of identity, but is open to conversion to the other for a reconciliation with the other. This basic law prevented Christianity from shutting itself up in a pre-established 'Hebrew truth' and enjoined it to seek its truth in its relationship with the other, the universal, the Greek, the Gentiles. This is what the theology of the second century did in allowing itself to be defined as faith in the Logos that the sages of Greece had been seeking for centuries, and this is what the New Covenant of Hebrew prophecy and Hellenistic culture fulfilled in its mixture of religiosity and philosophy, the royal way of the penetration of the gospel in the Greco-Roman world. In this respect, the 'culture mediation' which I have described represents the cost that had to be paid for the Gospel to come down to us and the debt of recognition that Christians of today owe to those of the first centuries for the boldness of such a test of truth.

This test has been fruitful, since its fruit has come down the centuries. But it continues in a quite new cultural context which it has to face with the same boldness. The Greek is knocking at our doors in the person of the immigrant without a country, the poor person without hope, the disenchantment of the ancient holy lands. The Gnostic apocalypses have become reality and block our horizons. We must always be converted to the other, the other who suffers. Stripped of myth, yesterday's truth, the same truth now has to be done in history.

Translated by John Bowden

Notes

1. For an analysis and assessment of talk of 'pre-existence' and Logos see my *L'homme qui venait de Dieu*, Paris 1993, 82–97.

2. Thus A. Grillmeier, *Christ in Christian Tradition*, Oxford [2] 1975, 27–35, 108–12.

3. Cf. J. Moingt, 'La reception du Prologue de Jean au IIe siècle', *RSCR* 83/2, 1995, 'Autour du Prologue de Jean', 249–82.

4. Cf. J. Moingt, *Théologie trinitaire de Tertullien*, Paris 1966–9, 894–5, 996–8, 1002–3.

5. Cf. Athenagoras, *Supplication*, 10.

6. Cf. again my *Théologie trinitaire de Tertullien* (n. 4), where I quote and analyse the texts to which I am alluding here: 183–224, 359–63, 1090–213, 1042–62.

The Limits of Christology or the Temptation to Absoluteness

Pierre Gisel

The figure of Jesus undeniably belongs at the heart of Christianity, as a historical reference, a central image and a theological context.

In connection with Jesus, Christian faith speaks of the 'incarnation of God'; it also speaks of the recapitulatory or archetypal figure of the human being ('new Adam' or 'Son of man'; he is the realization of the 'image of God'). Jesus has been called 'Christ' (i.e. literally 'Messiah'), the place and moment of revelation and, over and above that, mediator, radically even 'true God' and 'true man' according to the formulations of the first councils (notably Chalcedon in 451).

Here we shall be rethinking what is involved in this, seeking to identify the truth in its depths. As in all important human matters, there are risks here: the best always appears alongside the worst. And here it has to be said quite clearly, as my title indicates, that the worst is associated with a temptation to absoluteness. To think about the full and deep truth of the figure of Christ presupposes that one is clear about the limits of this figure and the way in which it is being referred to. In other words, christological truth presupposes that one has dissociated oneself from all christolatry and can see the very truth of what is being revealed, in relation to both God and human beings.

Here the approach will be one internal to Christianity. However, it must go hand in hand with a different, external approach, that characteristic of the history of religions.[1]

I Jesus: founder of Christianity or central point of reference for Christian faith?

I shall proceed by stating propositions, deliberately grafted on to the basic scriptural and doctrinal facts of Christianity,[2] without developing all their speculative scope.

The title of this section already indicates the first thesis or orientation: in my view the second term in the alternative formulated is the valid one, rather than the first.

According to the very logic of Christianity, Jesus is not its founder. He has not been presented in this way, nor does he function in this way: he is not seen strictly as a beginning, a figure who brings a special revelation of God to a group, a body or a people whose space and reality are separate and specific as such.[3]

To begin with, let us remember that Christianity is a religion of the book (there are different types of book, regardless of content: the Qur'an, which is in principle homogeneous; the Hebrew Bible, with its threefold division of Torah, Prophets and Writings, opening up on the Midrash and then the Talmud; the Christian Bible enclosed in its duality and the interplay of references[4] which arises from it). What have been canonized have been texts, texts of believers coming to grips with their identities and their own situations, and not the words of Jesus (thus the apocryphal sayings of Jesus have no canonical value, while by contrast the words put on to the lips of Jesus by the Bible which Jesus will not have spoken have full canonical value; at least if one passes, without really thinking about it, from a supposed fundamentalism of the text to an implicit fundamentalism of the person of Jesus).

Moreover, the text does not begin with the preaching or the work of Jesus and its sequel. It is twofold, Old Testament and New Testament, put canonically on the same footing (neither in religious nor theological terms does the New Testament replace or demote the Old Testament, as for example the Qur'an demotes all former texts, though these may contain historical facts and insights), though one is called 'Old' and the other 'New' (they are both canonical, but form a single unit).

To continue, the text comes first, with – as happens in every text and all literature – its expressions, memories and aims, the setting it gives to human beings and the world, its indirect indications and references to the beginning and the end. This is where the figure of Jesus is set down in writing and thus presented to us. This figure is the central reference, at the heart of a picture and a history. In fact Jesus is basically presented in terms of an ancient matrix (the 'christological' or 'messianic' matrix according to which his person, his work and his destiny have been received, reread and recognized). This matrix has rich symbolism (that of the scripture of the time, which was to become the Christian Old Testament): the figure of Moses, the figure of the prophet, the Davidic theme, apocalyptic features, the structures of festivals, Passover and Pentecost, and so on. There is an interplay of references behind the text, making them deeper and reshaping them ('hearts slow to believe', 'interpreting the scriptures' he showed them that 'it must be . . .', Luke 24.25–27), in which the ancient matrix is mobilized to welcome and understand the event of Jesus (hence the confession of Christ) and in which, reciprocally, the event of Jesus relaunches the ancient matrix (it is displaced and in part subverted once one claims a figure, Jesus Christ, as 'fulfilment', cf. Mark 1.15; John 19.28, 30).

Put in a central position (it plays a role as a recapitulatory[5] figure), the figure of Jesus from now on springs up again as a radical origin: the worlds will be said to be 'made' or 'created in Christ' (John 1.3; I Cor. 8.6; Col. 1.16; Heb. 1.2) and an equally radical end: the last secret of the world is unveiled in the 'name' of the 'witness' (cf. the Apocalypse).

To proceed yet further, here I have recalled and validated the fact of scripture: a fact of faith, of recapitulation, memory and attestation, active, affirmative and hopeful. At the same time, or in parallel, I would like to refer to the theme of covenant. Here is an overall structure from which the figure of Jesus must not be detached: on the contrary, it requires this framework and is involved in it, deeply.[6]

To talk of covenant in connection with the Bible is to talk of history, a history which unfolds. But this is not history as a formal framework or the neutral stage of a theatre, nor does it unfold in accordance with a strict linearity. The story of the covenant describes a process made up of experiences and happenings, of hurts and trials, intrigues and possible or actual transitions. Theologically, the covenant stems from a reciprocal election and nomination, one which includes law and exodus, exile and return. The covenant is the symbolic framework and structure in which the history of relations between God and human beings unfolds and expresses itself, the history of a creation which is taken up time and again. And here, in this framework and as its centre, Christ is regarded both as an unveiling of the scheme and as a paradigmatic figure. This figure is written into the creative process of God, a process which is constantly resumed, in the world and human beings, in the fact of evil (the cross) and in accordance with an original and final surplus (he is 'conceived by the Spirit'; God raises him and 'exalts him to his right hand').

Theologically, and strictly speaking, Christ is not an intermediary here (a mixed or hybrid 'nature', an exception to the common order); he is a place of revelation, his body and figure offered to the contemplation and appropriation of believers or as a place of mediation – quite specifically a body and a figure in which the human and the divine, the divine and the human, show themselves and intertwine.

II Jesus: the representative in place of God or the figure of a reference to God (to the 'Father' and the 'spirit')

Here, as in the first section, the heading suggests an alternative and here too the first term ('representative in place of God') will be rejected and the second endorsed ('figure of a relationship to God').

I have said that the person of Jesus is constructed and functions, in Christian terms, as a central point of reference. This is the way in which he is Jesus Christ. Discourse about him is secondary, of a lower order: it is religious discourse and the discourse of faith, or of non-faith. Theologically, the truth of the Jesus event is told only after the paschal mystery (after, and as a function of).[7] Christian discourse about Jesus is outside of contemporaneity, both in fact (Jesus is absent, dead to the world and raised to God) and by right (seeing the historical Jesus in the present, as an eye-witness, did not in itself lead to faith). In classical doctrine, it is in the Spirit that Jesus is recognized as Christ, relating to the Father.

The setting in the context of the Gospel and the believer confirms this overall disposition; it attests and illustrates it. Let us look at the key elements here, not forgetting that we have four Gospels set side by side which are very different in their narrative material and in the way in which they look at Jesus and therefore in their overall picture (and it should be added that this irreducible difference does not just affect the periphery but the central point of reference).

(a) Basic doublings

I would like to emphasize, first, that according to the Bible and for the believer, the point of reference is presented in terms of an origin irreducibly characterized by a doubling, and an end which is evoked according to the same procedure; the profound identity or the secret of the person in question is presented in terms of this origin and this end. There is coherence here, since the same figure who is the point of reference will be the object, this time at the centre of the narrative deployment (between the beginning and the end) of a presentation which reveals his profound identity or secret. This will take place through a transfiguration (Mark 9.2–8) which proclaims in relation to God ('A voice came out of the cloud, saying "This is . . ."', followed in v. 8, according to a procedure which recurs in the Gospels, cf. Luke 24.31, by a disappearance of that which might disclose, or which discloses only by transfiguration) a truth which is not visible historically and every day, and which moreover the disciples do not seem to understand, situated as they are on another level (cf. v. 5 'Let us make three booths . . .').

Let us look more closely at the origin, which I have said is a double one: 'flesh of Mary' and 'conceived of the Spirit'. This is a historical and human genealogy: born of David or of Adam (cf. Luke 3.38), 'son of man' or 'new Adam', and coming from God, by a break or vertically: 'son of God' or 'the Most High'. We find this basic religious disposition, *mutatis mutandis*, in the sequence of enthronement: baptism in solidarity with humanity (Matt. 3.15) and baptism in which the divine sonship is expressed ('this is my beloved son', Mark 1.11); withdrawal into the desert as a situation which at the same time is not human (v. 13, he is 'with the wild animals and the angels served him'); and the internal resumption of the destiny of Adam. In fact, theologically, the temptations of Jesus take up Gen. 3: as with the original Adam, for the new Adam the truth and the life come about according to the alternative of finitude: not to transform stones into bread and feed the crowds (which in itself would not seem to be a bad action or one to be condemned), and thus to live according to God (for Jesus this goes as far as the 'but not what I will' of Gethsemane, by way of the 'Get thee behind me, Satan' addressed to the prince of the apostles who thinks that Jesus could escape suffering and death), or on the contrary to want to be 'like the gods' (Gen. 3.5: the three temptations; the refusal to summon a 'legion of angels' at the arrest, Matt. 26.53) and in fact to take his place amidst lies and death.

Now let us look at the other pole, the end. That too is twofold, in many respects. First of all, and this is fundamental for our study, the fulfilment is a double one: a parousia according to the figure of the crucified Jesus (the Messiah has come and 'all is fulfilled', John 19.30) and a parousia according to the figure of Christ in glory. It is a doubling in accordance with the motif of a 'return' – everything is reported – or an eschatological ('apocalyptic') unveiling bound up with the fact that for Christians, though the Messiah has indeed come, the messianic kingdom is still an object of expectation and hope. In this context there is also a doubling – which is probably connected – between a Christic pole and a pneumatological pole: 'it is an advantage for you if I go' (John 16.7), bound to the announcement of the Spirit: 'and you will do the same works as I do, and even greater ones' (John 14.21).

We can and must go even deeper. At the pole of the end or fulfilment the reference figure expresses himself in the form of effacement and – in a different way – there comes the reality of a 'body of Christ' (the church). Jesus has to be handed over to the forces of death (to the human beings who crucify him, and through that to the sin to which he is assimilated, being 'made sin', II Cor. 5.21; Gal. 3.13, and to the hell to which he descends). There he links himself to a destiny which is going to be the mystery of life for believers ('we are baptized into his death', Rom. 6.3; Gal. 3.27, nurtured by his 'broken body'; I Cor. 11.24f.; 'we bear in our body the agony of Jesus', II Cor. 4.10; or the 'marks of Jesus', Gal. 6.17), whose bodies have been made the 'temple of the Holy Spirit' (I Cor. 6.19) and who, both free and objects of transfiguration 'into the image' of Christ, from 'glory to glory' (II Cor. 3.17f.), have to 'be born anew' (Gal. 4.19).

Let us go even deeper. The final point is not precisely an end, a decisive moment which could be isolated, and which would itself be a moment of revelation or fundamental salvation. Besides, for Christians, it is the cross that is said to be the moment of salvation. Now the cross is nothing without what goes before it and what comes after it (and what follows it and what precedes it is falsehood and nothingness without the cross). The final pole of the presentation of Jesus (without directly implying the 'apocalyptic' parousia here) is not an end; it is the Easter mystery (the fact of both the cross *and* the resurrection) *and* Pentecost (in which the difference of his truth will be articulated in life, and according to the Spirit), moreover by way of the Ascension.

(b) A revelation which appeals – discontinuously – to God

Let us return to the concrete setting of Jesus as a central point of reference, to emphasize the interplay of what is revealed there and thus the way in which Jesus can be said and confessed to be 'revelation' and 'mediation'.

First the cross. Except in the Johannine re-reading, which seems to me to be valid only as a re-reading which presupposes from beginning to end another story that is in the mind of believers (without this, taken by itself and without the references it makes, it can be seen understood only in Gnostic terms[8]), the death of Jesus is marked by betrayal, denial and abandonment. This is not Socrates taking the hemlock, surrounded by his friends and conversing with them. One of the Twelve, Judas, betrayed Jesus (apostolically he was to be replaced, according to a new initiative on the part of God, by Paul, who was neither one of the Twelve nor, strictly speaking, an eye-witness); the one who is designated the rock of the future church, Peter, denied Jesus despite the promises he gave; the other disciples fled. Jesus is 'handed over' to be killed in the name of the religious (Sanhedrin) and political (Pilate) authorities. He is thwarted ('save yourself') and cries out in despair to God ('my God, my God, why have you forsaken me?').

Then comes the resurrection. The resurrection is not depicted in the canonical Gospels (things are different in the apocryphal Gospel of Peter). It was spoken of after the event in terms of appearances and an empty tomb which were less proofs than elements which brought into play a process of memory and recognition (an identity beyond discontinuity and hetero-geneity), after an interval and through substitution (for example in Mark 6.1–8 a closed tomb full of the presence of a dead body was replaced by the proclamation at the place of a tomb which was open and said to be empty of a presence which 'goes before' into Galilee 'as he told you') or through an opposition between a presence incognito, under the sign of a failure, and an unveiling bound up with a withdrawal or an absence under the sign of a victorious and shared revival (for example, Luke 24.13–35).

Here is a double presentation – cross and resurrection – which shows less a continuity through faithfulness than a discontinuity: death is bound up at the extreme with a negativity, and the resurrection is neither a rebirth from death (death and negativity are not so much suppressed or minimized as revealed in their annihilating power, which is radically opposed to God), nor the revival of a dead body (the 'body' of the risen Jesus passes through walls, appears in different places regardless of distance, must not be 'touched',[9] and appears basically polarized on the Ascension[10]), nor the power of a hero victorious over death (it is more God who raises Jesus than Jesus who, by his own power of his 'merits', rises). The resurrection is a manifestation proclaiming contrary to the laws and evidence of the world and in opposition to the forces of sin a surplus of creative force in God.

Both the cross and the resurrection are places and moments of eschatological manifestation, the last according to the divine order, and thus radical or ruptured. This is true of both, and they form an irreducible complex. For Christians the resurrection does not eliminate the cross: the cross is not a bad moment to be passed but a moment of 'last' revelation, which thus retains its full relevance throughout time.

Finally, the concrete setting of the life of Jesus – of his ministry – is quite instructive. What are we shown? Jesus is the one who speaks in parables and thus according to the procedures of an 'indirect communication',[11] who shifts the focal point or twists the original questions rather than replying to them, who shows our reality in a different form rather than giving new and specific facts. He does not resolve the enigma. Similarly, Jesus is spoken of in connection with various encounters which are also surprising: they take a strange course, and the words exchanged often have a double meaning.

Jesus is still presented as one who does miracles, healings in particular, not without a link to the social games which imprison people ('possessions'), and offering signs of a lordship which differs from the laws of the world. Miracles exist (but one can do miracles 'by Beelzebul', and 'magicians' like Simon also do miracles), but they are not decisive as such (they are not demonstrations which draw crowds), and above all are basically ambivalent (cf. John 6.15, 26: the crowds seek Jesus because they have 'seen' the miracle of the bread but have missed the truth, precisely because of that). For the Gospel, miracle is nothing (the question of what it reveals, where it comes from and to what it relates is basically open) or is the wrong proof (above all when it is seen for itself).

Jesus is equally spoken of in terms of a whole fabric of relationships. Quite apart from the disciples, who have already been mentioned (they do not understand, or only understand afterwards),[12] there are the marginal people, poor in various ways, rejected or transgressors (women, Samaritans, prostitutes, toll-collectors, the occupying forces and so on). Jesus is generally presented in a typology which contrasts him with the Pharisees, the heroes of an absolute faithfulness to the law (the law of God). Paul takes up this motif and makes it central; Jesus crucified in the name of the Law opens up a new world (a 'new creation', II Cor. 5.17). And if Jesus teaches, it is in tension with Moses (cf. the Sermon on the Mount, Matt. 5–7) or in a way resembling the prophets who were not recognized (cf. Luke 4.16–30).[13]

(c) Conclusion

The figure of Christ belongs within a messianic matrix, but it subverts this matrix, radicalizing both the question of God and that of the destiny of the world. Revelation is there,[14] but the revelation is indirect, and it works on the body and the figure which are offered or put forward: not only in what Jesus says and does, but even more in what he is made to undergo.

III A reflective summary

The temptation to absoluteness is that of isolating the figure of Jesus Christ to make it a reality that one commits oneself to, in and for itself. In that case it no longer reveals and it is no longer mediation. Positively, the figure of Christ must be subjected to the only questions which are legitimate in this connection: that of God (his identity and his truth) and that of the human (his identity and truth). Without this, Christ becomes a substitute for God (he becomes an ideal) or a superman (a fantasy). Far from leading us to God (to the surplus over and above all reality and truth which he represents) or being the way to God, he closes up the human space of questioning and experience. Conversely, far from resorting to the human structuration of belief, with its symbolic and spiritual facts written on the heart of the world,[15] the figure of Christ leads to a 'sacrifice' of its real properties. This double temptation lurks at the innermost depth of Christianity.

The force of Christianity is that it has radicalized the question of God and God's relationship to the world:[16] the reality and truth of God are not separate from the world and human beings but decisively involved. So one can say that revelation pertains to that which is 'peculiar' to God, without losing its character or changing (hence the notion of an eternal, 'uncreated' 'sonship' or 'engendering'), one from all times and for all times. Theologically this was to commit oneself to a vision in which the divine (the reality and the truth of God) is not only at the heart of the 'principle' (the Father, or the Creator alone?), but 'determines' it in a concrete and peculiar way, taking it from the heart of the world and putting it into effect.[17]

That was what was achieved at Nicaea (325) against Arius. It is valid at the level of our understanding of God (and, bound up with that, of humanity). It aimed to go beyond the confession of God as a 'common genre' by presenting God's 'nature', 'substance' or 'essence' subverted, brought together and made concrete by 'persons' (or 'hypostases') who were said to subsist in God.

We can see what happens in christology. It was thought possible from the reflexive or speculative truth of Nicaea (a level of truth which in my view is unmistakable, provided that it is made precise), to trace a linear way downwards (wrongly: this was in fact to confuse the ontological – reflective and speculative – and historical – existential, figurative or hermeneutical – orders). The christological formulae show this; here we find a recurrent difficulty, that of assuring the full humanity of Christ (Chalcedon), including his own will (Constantinople III, 7891).[18] In other words, Jesus is not God, and this is a fact that must always be remembered at the heart of the Christian faith.[19]

Epilogue

I have not put any emphasis here on the 'historical Jesus'.[20] Nevertheless the space for work and meditation was basically historical, though the question is one of the history of belief and its representations. That is why actual Christianity and the faith bound up with it have been the focus here. In my view, that is the only adequate place for theological reflection.

Notes

1. According to a perspective which can appeal to Ernst Troeltsch, the classical detective of absoluteness in modernity.

2. Certainly they have a historical and cultural stamp and are not valid for themselves; I take them as indicative and symptomatic, relating to a specific religious profile.

3. Of course Christianity means speaking the truth about God and human beings, globally.

4. In this game there is an indirect but decisive reference to Christ as a figure outside the text and one that is spoken of (put in place).

5. For the Fathers, Christ recapitulates the destiny of creation.

6. Calvin strongly emphasized it, in contrast to Luther, on the basis of the break from the scholastic legacy which began from the eternal generation of the Son in God. I emphasize this in my book *Le Christ de Calvin*, Paris 1990.

7. This is the element of truth which Rudolf Bultmann constantly emphasized.

8. Which is what Ernst Käsemann feared.

9. Cf. John 20.17. Even Thomas does not touch him but prostrates himself in adoring recognition.

10. It is no coincidence that this time is forty days.

11. The expression is Kierkegaard's. Nietzsche will speak of the 'madman', the one 'without a place' who illuminates the world.

12. As for Mary, she is hardly present (except in the Johannine account of the cross), and the actual narrative does not presuppose that the miracle of the virginal conception (a perpetual virginity seems to me more of a deviation than an illumination) and the marvels of Christmas remain stamped on her heart (cf. Matt. 13.54–58). Generally speaking, if it is impossible to write a Christian Gospel without the story of the cross and the resurrection, it can be written without the virgin birth, cf. Mark (and, partially at least, John).

13. The text of the Transfiguration shows Moses and Elijah (the type of the prophet) beside Jesus.

14. Let us recall that Pannenberg proposed to make this a central motif.

15. This is the importance of a correct and strong doctrine of the Spirit.

16. That is the effect of the 'apocalyptic motive' which reappears in the theme of the 'incarnation' and the affirmation of the 'Trinity'.

17. Classically, but a Latin and modern trend (both Roman Catholic and Protestant) have lost sight of this. It is a matter of honouring not only the 'communication' from the Father to the Son (and then to believers), i.e. salvation, but even more the reciprocity or the return, from the Son to the Father (and from believers to God).

18. Against monothelitism: the second person does not act directly in Jesus as if it had taken the place of his own will; Jesus is man and prays to God.

19. That is why in doctrine I prefer to think of the figure of Christ as the body and matter of salvation rather than as his agent: it is God who gives salvation.

20. In other words, the 'historical Jesus' has no theological relevance as such; emphasizing him (except as an initial stage which makes it possible to specify the status of an affirmation of belief) can only serve, consciously or not, to reverse a theism which is not unscathed by christological fantasies.

Christology and the Paschal Imagination

Richard G. Cote

To the question 'Who do you say I am?' Christians of every age and every culture have responded with a profession of faith that is at once steeped in the living tradition of the church as well as in their own religious imagination. The role and play of imagination in every act of faith, but especially when assenting to and professing the identity and mission of Christ, will be the focus of this article.

Theologians have been slow to recognize the creative imagination as a central component not merely in the 'human response' of faith but also in the very structure which evokes faith. Until quite recently they have virtually ignored the play of imagination even in the construction of their own christologies. This comes as no surprise since the West, for the greater part of its intellectual history, has given pride of place to reason, not imagination. Post-Cartesian philosophers and psychologists belittled the imaginative quality of human life, at best relegating it to assorted groups like artists and poets, at worse regarding it as a deception and dangerous power. The church, too, has distrusted imagination and excluded imaginal experience (creativity, theopoesis, playfulness) from much of its sanctioned vision of reality and magisterial teaching. An extreme mistrust of imagination, for example, can be seen in the way Pascal regarded it as a spiritual deceiver: 'It is man's ruling faculty, queen of lies and error, and all the greater deceiver since she does not always deceive . . . But being most often false she leaves no sure mark of her quality, for she sets the same stamp upon truth and falsehood.'[1]

Even in Western aesthetics, up until the eighteenth century, the artist was regarded primarily as a craftsman-like *imitator* of nature and the human mind, a mirror that simply reflects external reality. A transformation in the status of imagination came about with Kant and the German idealists, for whom the synthesizing power of imagination was seen as central to human understanding, the way it frames and shapes into a unity its own image of reality. Instead of being a 'mirror' merely reflecting external nature, the mind was regarded now as a 'lamp' which radiates its own inner light on to the objects it perceives.[2] Imagination was no longer viewed simply as a 'reproductive' faculty, but as a productive or creative power both in the acquisition of knowledge and in the production of art. Thus for the Romantic poets and their successors imagination came to be seen (and so described by Baudelaire) as 'the queen of the faculties', 'the queen of truth'.

Despite the avowed mistrust of imagination in the West generally, and in the church of the West in particular, ironically religious imagination has always played an important role in the life of faith, especially when faith 'seeks understanding' (theology). At no time did Christians ever completely lose or eradicate the imaginative dimension of their faith, even in those periods of history when it must have seemed quite unorthodox to view imagination as essential to a life of faith. On the contrary, they seem always to have known – and indeed known with the sure instinct of their faith (*sensus fidelium*) – that the vital point of contact between divine revelation and human experience is the imagination, our natural, inborn faculty for transcendence. This is especially evident throughout the history of the church both in the popular piety and devotions of the faithful and in the Christian mystical tradition of the West. At either end of the Christian spectrum – whether at the grassroots level of the church or at the sublime heights of such mystics as Hugh of St Victor, Bernard of Clairvaux, Ruysbroeck, John of the Cross, Teresa of Avila – the active imagination of Christians in every age has survived with remarkable splendour (if at times somewhat marginally) in the life of the church.

In an original and highly regarded study, *Jesus Through the Centuries*, Jaroslav Pelikan has shown how Christians have variously imagined Jesus in each successive epoch – from rabbi in the first century to King of kings in the fourth to universal man in the Renaissance to liberator in the nineteenth and twentieth centuries. Not only does this study shed light on the temper and values of Western society in various epochs but it also provides good insight into the way in which the collective imagination of Christians works and is creatively active at any given time. That a predominant image or symbol or metaphor of Jesus prevails in any given century is a sure sign of the church's active imagination, the way it seeks to discern the 'signs of the times' in order to give an ever new, more contemporary response to the question 'Who do you say I am?'.

At the level of faith, this recomposing or repatterning of Christ's image by the imagination is what makes him still beautiful and meaningful for us today. The transcendent play of Christian imagination consists in 'seeing' beyond what meets the eye – including beyond the *literary* Jesus of the gospel text. It is a 'to-and-fro' re-visioning, a re-interpretation of the connection between the risen and glorified Lord *and* 'our times', and 'our world'. From the point of view of the church's faithful imagination there is a constant 'going back and forth' between the Christ in glory and the faithful on earth so as to order a new pattern, a new way of 'seeing' the whole. Whether the repatterning be dramatic or subtle, epochal or short-lived, the reordering of the particular is invariably a repatterning of the whole. Though not the first, Samuel Taylor Coleridge (1772–1834) identified imagination as the composing activity of the mind, the power of shaping and unifying into a whole (*Einbildungskraft*). He was also one of the first to discern and posit a real bond between faith and imagination – understanding both as shaping and unifying activities which are constitutive of being human as well as being a believer in 'eternal truths'. Faith, for Coleridge, like imagination in poetry, must be an energy of the whole person. It involves a venture, almost a wager, embarked upon with only the assurance of things hoped for, and 'believing where we cannot prove'.

The nature of imagination

In order fully to appreciate the crucial role that the paschal, or Christian, imagination plays in the construction of any and all christologies (and they are legion!), a few further clarifications about imagination may be helpful. First, it should be pointed out that although the imagination is a constructive, image-making faculty, this must not be understood in an exclusive visual sense. As Mary Warnock has rightly pointed out, the meaningful 'form' which the imagination generates may be a mental image in some cases, but quite often it is not.[3] The form may, for example, consist in a structure or web of ideas to which we cannot attach a particular picture. Or again, as in the case of music, it could be a structure of sounds instead of a visual or intellectual structure. This is why Garrett Green has preferred to describe imagination, not as the image-making faculty, but rather as the paradigmatic (pattern-making and pattern-recognizing) faculty. '*Pattern*,' he says, 'though generally connoting visual experience, is more abstract than *image* and less dependent on visual metaphor.'[4]

Second, it should be emphasized that the imagination connects us to things and the world around us in more than an intellectual or visual way; the forms or images it produces are *loaded with affect*. Paul Ricoeur has explored the implications of this by connecting metaphors with moods and feeling. The imagination works out of an environment or network of relationship, within which we live and move and become the persons we are. Feelings, Ricoeur contends, have an ontological bearing: 'Through feeling we find ourselves already located in the world.'[5] As David Bryant explains:

> The full significance of this comes to light when we think of feelings not primarily as personal emotions, such as the inner experience of joy or fear, but as our way of belonging to and participating in the world . . . Thus the forms through which we understand the world, and which carry *the feelings that intimately connect us to the world*, are able to disclose possible ways of participating in the world.[6]

This affective 'embeddedness' in the world applies to all our human environments, be it family, culture or religion. It projects us not only intellectually into deeper understanding of a situation, but also affectively and emotionally into it. Bryant illustrates this in the religious sphere with the symbol of the Kingdom of God. To Christians for whom this symbol carries a certain significance, the Kingdom of God refers first of all to what God has done and continues to do in the world to achieve the divine purpose. Yet at the same time it makes certain modes of participation in the world meaningful for Christians, that is, special determined ways of being involved that correspond to God's act. And it does this, moreover, at a level that relates to our pre-reflective and affective involvement in the world, as well as to our rational involvement. As a symbol, therefore, the Kingdom of God makes a claim on the lives of Christians and its power is rooted, as with all living symbols, in the power of the imagination. In other words, the imagination has a catalytic effect, provoking the depiction and aiding, through imaginative representations, the appropriation of new ways of being in the world. It is in and through our imagination that this new way of being is brought to our attention.

Third, imagination not only has a catalytic effect but also has the power to generate meaning. In *The Rule of Metaphor* and in various articles, Ricoeur situates the role of the imagination in a dynamic hermeneutics. He shows how metaphoric language, as an 'impertinent predication', has the uncanny ability to shatter both the previous structures of our language *and* the previous structures of what we call reality, thereby giving us new insight into reality. What metaphors enable us to see is not the world whose meaning we previously thought we knew, but the world whose possibilities for existence suddenly become meaningful for us in a new and revitalized way.

The 'parabolic imagination' of Jesus is a case in point.[7] The projection of new possibilities is clearly evident in the way Jesus 'sees' the Kingdom of God as a sower . . . a mustard seed . . . a budding fig tree . . . a watchman . . . a lost sheep . . . a hidden treasure . . . a pearl . . . a good Samaritan . . . a prodigal son, etc. The parables of Jesus are especially helpful in our discussion for several reasons. First, Jesus' parables enshrine for us a particularly reliable part of the Christian tradition; with them, we have the assurance, in the logic of exegetical probability, that we are in contact with the historical Jesus and with what Sandra M. Schneiders calls the 'world behind the text'. Second, Jesus' metaphorical discourse on the Kingdom is not simply the reiteration or even the amplification of some past event or reality. It refers us to a new way of 'seeing' reality with its hitherto undisclosed human possibilities. This constitutes a creative moment for us (Ricoeur calls it an event[8]) that breaks open the future rather than the past alone. In this important respect, Jesus' metaphorical speech coincides with the 'inbreaking' of that reality we call the Kingdom of God. His parables would have us think the unthinkable, conceive the inconceivable, and imagine the unimaginable, namely, the real possibility of 'a new heaven and a new earth'. And finally, as we will now consider, Jesus' way with metaphoric language establishes imagination as an authentic theological category. Even Saint Thomas, in a remarkable text in which he shows how theology is a work of art, says that theology 'ought to be expressed in a manner that is metaphorical, that is, symbolic or parabolic'.[9]

The paschal imagination in theology

If human imagination is our natural, inborn faculty for transcendence, for going 'beyond' what we call reality, that is, beyond what hitherto seemed real and possible, the faithful imagination of Christians opens up unprecedented possibilities of reinterpretation and hence new possibilities of existence. It was Sandra M. Schneiders, I believe, who first coined the expression 'paschal imagination' in reference to the way the first Christians imaginatively constructed a unified whole (the paschal paradigm) from three very distinct realities: (a) the *actual* Jesus (the 'world behind the text'); (b) the *literary* Jesus (the 'world of the text'); and (c) the *proclaimed* Jesus (the 'world before the text'), the latter being encoded in the witness character of the New Testament text. Schneiders explains:

> The paschal mystery of Jesus . . . is itself an imaginative construct. The unified whole that we call the paschal mystery contains elements that are genuinely historical (such as Jesus' death on the cross) and events that are transhistorical (such as the resurrection) and interpretation through biblical categories spoken of in physical language (such as ascent to God's right hand). This integration of historical experience with faith experience creates the tensive image of the 'paschal mystery of Jesus' by which the diverse elements are integrated into a single reality.[10]

This paradigmatic construct is the product of the faith-filled imagination of the first Christians: the way they envisaged the actual (both earthly and glorified) Jesus as the Christ and presented that image in literary-historical form in order to elicit the faith response of the hearer/reader.[11]

What makes the risen Christ still believable and trustworthy for present-day Christians, even though we live some two thousand years 'after' Christ, is the exercise of this same paschal imagination. As a constitutive component of faith itself, the paschal imagination is what makes the present-day believer a *real* 'contemporary disciple' of Christ, with claims upon us as immediate as when the historical Jesus spoke to the Samaritan woman at the well, or to the Pharisees or to Peter. It also gives transcendent actuality to St Paul's statements about our being already raised in Christ. This is what can be called the *contemporanizing* function of the paschal imagination: it renders the past-as-present and the future-as-inchoate (i.e., already begun), thereby giving present-day believers an immanent sense of Christ's *real presence* in the world today.

This aspect of the paschal imagination in fact became the cornerstone of the sacramental theology developed in the Middle Ages. Thus St Thomas could attribute a triple dimension to the sacramental sign. A sacrament, he says, is at once *commemorative* of the past (the Passion of Christ), *demonstrative* of what is actually effected in us (grace), and being *prognostic* of future glory (*ST* III, 60, 3). Such a symbolic construct, combining as it does three different realities in a single sacramental 'economy,' is again but the theological product of the paschal imagination.

Another example of the paschal imagination at work, especially in its interpretative capacity, can be seen in the typological method of interpreting Scripture familiar to many earlier generations of Christians. In its interpretative role, the paschal imagination establishes historical connections between certain events, persons or things in the Old Testament and similar events, persons or things in the New Testament – connections that would otherwise almost certainly be overlooked or missed. As a method of exegesis, typology correlates passages in the Old Testament which foreshadow, hint at, or openly predict things fulfilled in the New Testament. Thus a coherent pattern is discerned in God's dealings with his people and this in turn discloses the inner meaning of the text and exhibits the correspondence of types and prophecies with their fulfilment. As St Augustine succinctly put it: 'In the Old Testament the New lies hid; in the New Testament the meaning of the Old becomes clear.'

The paschal imagination is especially crucial for the church today if it is to speak at all meaningfully to our modern world. Because of the enormous distance that separates us from the biblical statements and the socio-cultural context in which they were orginally cast, it is not enough simply to 'adapt' the content of the New Testament to our contemporary society and culture. What is needed today, as in every new age and culture, is nothing less than a *creative reinterpretation* of Christianity itself. This means that a new language and discourse of faith must be found that will successfully bridge the cultural time-lag between the fundamental experience and testimony of the New Testament on the one hand, and our own present-day human experience and attitudes on the other. This can only be done through a bold act of creative reinterpretation, the kind of creative act of which only the paschal imagination is capable. That such a creative undertaking has already begun can be seen, for example, in the recent concerted effort among theologians to develop a theology of *inculturation* and new models of contextual theology.

As a pattern-making and pattern-recognizing faculty, the paschal imagination has always been active among theologians and perdures to this day. One does not need to plunge very deeply into the history and development of christology in order to sense just how instrumental this faculty has been in the construction of christologies throughout the centuries. Christology, like theology itself, is, and will always be, an imaginative construction.[12] We see evidence of this in the first century: the Johannine christology is very different from Mark's christology, Q christology is very different from that of Luke and Matthew, and there is even diversity of interpretation as to what the victory of Jesus was. We also see this in the profound paradigm shifts that have taken place in christology in recent years – the shift, for example, from a 'Christ with two natures' to a 'Christ without duality' (Schoonenberg); from a christology 'from above' to a christology 'from below' (Küng); from an 'onto-' christology to a 'functional' christology (Sobrino); from christology as an autonomous treatise in dogmatic theology to one that is interlaced and intertwined with creation (Rahner), with the Trinity (H. Balthasar), and with politics (Metz). In recent years, there has been a proliferation of 'local theologies' that take culture and cultural change seriously and this, too, has led to various new *models* of contextual theology and hence new interpretations of the figure of Christ.[13] In North American biblical scholarship alone, no less than six major new portraits of Jesus have emerged in the past sixteen years.[14]

What all this means is what Hans Urs von Balthasar has aptly demonstrated in his masterwork, *The Glory of the Lord*, namely, how utterly and enduringly attractive the revelation of God in Christ really is. When we begin to 'see' the inherent beauty of what God has done in Christ, his greatest 'work of art' (as Gadamer might say), then there can be no limit, no end, to the imaginative representations of Christ which the faithful will envisage and entertain. Until the end of time, the Christian imagination will generate ever new paradigms in the hope of forever capturing something more, something else, of the splendour and radiance of this unfathomable mystery.

Notes

1. B. Pascal, *Pensées*, translated by H. F. Stewart, London 1950, 39.
2. See M. H. Abrams, *The Mirror and the Lamp: Romantic Theory and the Critical Tradition*, New York 1953.
3. See Mary Warnock, *Imagination*, Berkeley and Los Angeles 1976, 152–60.
4. Garrett Green, *Imagining God: Theology and the Religious Imagination*, New York 1989, 94.
5. Paul Ricoeur, 'Creativity in Language', in *Philosophy Today* 17(2/4), 1973, 111; see also Ricoeur, *Interpretation Theory: Discourse and Surplus of Meaning*, Fort Worth, TX 1976, 59–60.
6. David J. Bryant, *Faith and the Play of Imagination: On the Role of Imagination in Religion*, Macon GA 1989, 204–5. Italics added.
7. See John McIntyre, *Faith, Theology and Imagination*, Edinburgh 1987, 19–39.
8. Ricoeur, *Interpretation* (n. 5), 91–2.
9. '*unde oportet modum istius scientiae esse metaphoricum, sive symbolicum, vel parabolicum*', in I Sent. Prol., q. I, a.v.
10. Sandra M. Schneiders, *The Revelatory Text: Interpreting the New Testament as Sacred Scripture*, San Francisco 1991, 105. See also Schneiders, 'The Paschal Imagination: Objectivity and Subjectivity in New Testament Interpretation', in *Theological Studies* 43, 1982, 52–68.
11. Ibid., 101; see also 'The Paschal Imagination', 66.
12. Gordon D. Kaufman, *The Theological Imagination. Constructing the Concept of God*, Philadelphia 1981, 263–79.

13. See Stephen B. Bevans, *Models of Contextual Theology*, Maryknoll, NY 1992.

14. Marcus J. Borg, 'Portraits of Jesus', in *The Search for Jesus: Modern Scholarship looks at the Gospels*, Washington, DC 1994, 83–103.

III · Following Jesus Today to God's Reign

The Identity of the Christian following Jesus Christ

Anne Fortin-Melkevik

The identity of the Christian encountering Jesus Christ

Theologies of identity now touch on all sectors of theological reflection and raise the question of encounter with the figure of Jesus Christ. In this respect the writings on Christian identity are legion, and the fertility of Paul Ricoeur's concept of narrative identity in theology no longer needs to be demonstrated. The human subjects who take up the story of their lives, who re-read the course of their existence in the light of their encounter with Jesus Christ, are thus put at the centre of a number of theologies. In so doing one gives priority to the way which retraces in the Bible stories that address the stories of our contemporaries.

The interest in quests for identity seems to indicate the urgent need to respond to a cry: Who am I in this church? Who am I in this society? However, these questions about the nature of humanity are not peculiar to theology. In the social sciences and in philosophy the concept of identity marks the recent works of several leading figures: Anthony Giddens, Alain Touraine, Charles Taylor, Jürgen Habermas and Paul Ricoeur, to mention only the best known. This end-of-century period is seeking to retrace the conditions of human identity at the political, social, cultural and religious levels. Thus theologians are sharing the most vital preoccupation of the hour. It remains to be discovered how theologies fit into this context.

However, before developing interpretative theories of identity, it is necessary to pause on the very conditions of interpretation. In fact the conditions of interpretation find a place in plural situations of interpretation which must be allowed their rights within theologies. What is at issue here is the very principle of theological reason. Does this reason allow respect for the human in its relationship of fundamental otherness; does it allow a plurality of interpretations in the community? How can the transition from Christian identity to the identity of the Christian be guaranteed? How can it be possible to go beyond a theology which gives an abstract definition of a Christian identity towards theologies which leave room for several identities of people who call themselves Christians within the communities? It is in connection with these questions that theological reason is staking its credibility in our contemporary world, since Christians are no longer seeking the point of reference for their identity in one institution; Christians are not in search of Christian identity or the identity of Christianity. The quest for identity is first of all personal and will therefore take on a narrative colouring. The challenge to be met if theological reason is to be made audible consists today in articulating the narrative quests of individuals for identity with propositions about community identity which can be fed by these individual quests, and which therefore will be plural. The move from a problematic of Christian identity to the identity of the Christian is more than a bit of flirting; the paradigm of pluralism within the community is at stake. That is why this transition from Christian identity to the identity of the Christian is increasingly important in the local churches. However, conflicts arise in the transition from a narrative identity defined individually to an argumentative identity open on the community.

That having been said, one of the strictly hermeneutical contexts of the challenge to the interpretation of identity today consists in a confrontation with the biblical texts. These texts do not in fact provide us with the identity of a historical Jesus or of the model Christian, but rather summon us to the interpretation of a Jesus who is *told* about and of the Christian reader. The interpretative act can no longer be limited to a historical reconstruction or a narrative theory in order to establish a bond between the text and the reader. If language is conceived of as the place of human structuration, if it is recognized as the way in which relations are built between human beings, it will be more than just an instrument for transmitting a message. The text does not aim only at transmitting information, at developing knowledge or a meaning that the subject will appropriate in his or her own way. The quest for the meaning of a text cannot be a simple automatic process of decoding; rather, the reader is brought into a relationship with the text as the subject of interpretation. This subject of the interpretation does not apply a given meaning to his or her life; before the moment of appropriating meaning there is the element of constructing the meaning that the text can have for the reader.

There are several possible ways of approaching the question of the identity of the Christian encountering Jesus Christ. The way I have chosen will be that of the act of reading the text, how one reads a text, on what presuppositions, and how the identity of the reader is established in and by this act of reading. First of all I shall present two conceptions of the conditions for interpreting identity by reading a text about the identity of Jesus, Mark 8.26–33. Then as a second stage we shall examine these conditions for interpreting the identity of Jesus in connection with the conditions of interpreting narrative identity and community identity.

The conditions for interpreting the identity of Jesus: Mark 8.27–33, 'Who do you say that I am?'

Two conceptions of the interpretative act will be presented in connection with reading the text of Mark 8.27–33. The conditions of interpreting identity will then be brought out. Two theories of meaning will be developed: (*a*) a theory of meaning in terms of sign-reference; (*b*) a theory of meaning to be constructed.

(a)   Meaning as sign-reference

The interpretation of Mark 8.29 can make Peter's reply to Jesus' question ('But who do you say that I am?' 'You are the Christ') an exemplary confession of faith. Peter's reply is then conceived of as an affirmation, a statement that the Christian is called on to repeat after Peter. The Christian identity would then be the endorsement of Peter's certitude of faith, the inclusion of the Christian world in the word of the disciple. In that case the identity of Jesus would not be a problem:[1] from the sign to the content, from the signifier to the signified, the continuity would be linear and uninterrupted. The messianic identity is expressed, and does not even have to be decoded: it offers itself immediately. The christologies of the titles are based on such an interpretation, often relying on the exploitation of isolated verses.

Furthermore one can put this v. 29 back in its context and see it as a criticism of an inconsistent saying about the identity of Jesus. In fact, Peter's confession is partial, since in his decoding of the signifier Christ, the external referent is inadequate. Peter interprets the signifier Christ by a triumphal referent, and then Jesus criticizes this referent for being inadequate. Consequently the reader of this passage would be invited not to adopt an incomplete referent under the signifier of Christ. Peter is then the counter-example of a confessing saying, since he wants to imprison the identity of Jesus in his own short-sighted views.

In these two interpretations, the interpretative process is analogous: a signified is attached to the signifier, an external referent to the sign. Whether Peter is considered a model or anti-model of the confession of faith, the same ploy of referring to an external signified conditions the reading. The reader must receive and appropriate the meaning which is already there, the meaning which imposes itself. The interpretative issue consists in isolating a verse or restoring it to its context; but in both cases the aim is to provoke in the reader the same true confession towards Jesus. In that case the appropriation of the meaning will construct the Christian identity in a unilateral way: the course of the word has already been traced and there is nothing more to do than to involve oneself in it. The validation of the interpretation would then depend on the human flourishing which resulted from it. Christian identity and human flourishing: the notions of identity and flourishing relate to abstract entities: i.e. Christian and humanity. What is the role of the individual in such a scenario? We may postulate that it will find its flourishing and its identity by basing itself on such abstract entities, by conforming to a model external to itself. The interpretative plurality comes down to the plurality of appropriations of one and the same meaning by different subjects, since the meaning is already there and imposes itself by offering itself directly.

(b)   The construction of meaning

The question 'Who do men say that I am' is met by a list of signifiers: 'John the Baptist, others say Elijah; others, one of the prophets.' This chain is followed by a new question: 'And you, who do you say that I am?' In place of a list of signifiers, just one is proposed: 'You are the Christ.'

However, it has to be noted that Jesus does not sanction any reply and does not give any approval. Rather, he commands the disciples not to speak of him to anyone, not to repeat any of these replies to people. In the teaching on the 'Son of man' the replies to the questions are then suspended. So reference of the identity of Jesus to the figure of Christ is not regarded as being 'the right answer', since Jesus the agent does not integrate it into his teaching on the 'Son of man'. Rather, the teaching of Jesus displaces the lines of references suggested by the answers by putting itself within the breach opened up by the inadequacy of the replies to the questions. The teaching of Jesus sets against 'sign' replies, the meaning of which is to be decoded immediately, a reply in the order of doing. The 'Son of man' is presented by Jesus not as a sign to be decoded on the basis of prior knowledge but rather as being set in a narrative context, in a story which brings out actions still to come. The repetition of the question of Jesus thus seems to do away with given replies, to propose another type of reply: one can either put a label on Jesus, reify his identity in a signifier or a list of signifiers, or break up the sign relationship to put the naming of identity in a narrative programme.

In that case the identity of Jesus is constructed in those actions which imply a series of transformations. Jesus then is not reduced to an ontological state, to a title which establishes a fixed identity for all eternity; Jesus puts his reply, rather, in an identity which is constructed in and by a series of transformations. The suspension of an immediate meaning is important because the meaning will be perceptible only after the event: the meaning will have to be reconstructed, recognized after the realization of the narrative programme which is still potential. We understand that Jesus commands them 'strictly' not to speak of him to anyone under the mode of a fixed identity: these replies were reductive, deduced *a priori* from an established knowledge. The identity decoded in this way would not leave room for any transformation, any suffering, any choice. That was not the way by which the meaning of Jesus' identity was to reach people's ears. Such a given sense, imposing itself as a saying outside all action, would go against the general intepretative approach of the Gospels. The reply given by Jesus implies that each person has to reconstruct the meaning on the basis of his interpretation of events. The sign refused to the Pharisees (Mark 8.11–13) follows this same logic: Jesus is asked for a sign reference, a sign to be decoded immediately, and he refuses to give one. The acts of multiplying the breads (Mark 8.1–9) were not sign references; they asked to be interpreted, to be understood (Mark 8.14–21). Rather than calling for an appropriation of meaning already there, Jesus indicates the interpretative task that the disciples have to undertake. They have to leave the immediate meaning (the disciples had only one loaf in the boat) so that their eyes are open to see and their ears can finally understand the meaning of the multiplication of the loaves. The disciples would be in a privileged position to enter into an interpretative relationship towards Jesus, but they do not yet understand the interpretative work which is implied in the relationship to him. The 'Who am I?' is enunciated in an interpretative relationship to doing: by contrast the Pharisees and the disciples are reducing identity to a sign cut off from action.

The conflict between the silence imposed on the disciples (v. 30) and Jesus' language about the Son of man spoken of openly (v. 32) confirms this hypothesis: there is no danger of speaking openly a language which calls for interpretation, a language which demands of the one who receives it work on the 'meaning of meaning'. On the contrary, there is a danger of propagating a closed discourse, a discourse which imprisons the one who receives it in a limiting knowledge. The glimpses of God should not be limiting, and they should not negate the course to be taken, since the very logic of the incarnation relates to the involvement of the Word of God in the course of human actions. Jesus as Word of God is thus understood as the language of God, as that which produces mediation between God and the human being. If Jesus is a 'sign' who does not give himself as an immediate sign reference, it is his life and death that are put into speech to interpret. To take the life and death of Jesus as signs which relate immediately to a known referent would prevent us quite simply from understanding the resurrection as a result of this very precise life and death. What place could there be for the resurrection in a reading which thought it had exhausted the meaning of the life and death of Jesus? Moreover, that is the problem of the disciples: they do not immediately grasp the resurrection, since they need a long interpretative process (Luke 24.13–53) in order finally to see, grasp and understand (Mark 8.21).

The identity of the reader

The identity of the reader can be constructed in the course of this suspension of meaning. God's respect for human freedom shows itself in the fact that it is our eyes, our ears and our heart which are addressed in an interpretative process. The meaning does not present itself immediately; the significance that a text could have for a reader awaits the act of reading, the involvement of the reader here and now.[2] So the meaning has to be constructed by each reader, and cannot be built up without the involvement of eyes, ears and heart. The potential way of Christian identity will thus be opened up by the act of reading, just as the gestures and words open up a meaning which is original in that one had not yet arrived at it. This way has not yet been taken, and to follow Jesus implies recognizing one's Christian identity in the actions still to come, to put oneself in suspense towards one's own identity, in relation to which one can only hope for a positive outcome.

So it is that the interpretation of the self, the text, and the tradition come together in the act of reading. From the readers' point of view, distancing, differentiation and a differentiated relationship to the text and experience bring openness to themselves and to others. The interpretations of other readers will be so many openings to the plurality of the text and the plurality of the interpretative tradition which break open a closed meaning. The readings will be validated by the many forms which the flourishing of the human beings can assume and in the thousand faces of Christian maturity. It will no longer be possible to reduce the identity of Jesus to knowledge, since Jesus is the language of God. The proximity of God and humanity will come about through the language which is the story of the life of Jesus.

So to read and interpret the text, the tradition and its narrative identity will be ways of stating and confessing one's faith in turn. Language constructs the identity of the reader in respect of the identity of Jesus in relation to the action to come. The maturity of the Christian consists in living in freedom, outside a fixed and given interpretation: the construction of interpretation implies daring to risk oneself – along with others – in the quest for meaning.

Thus the relationship with the text implies a real encounter of otherness: the text offers ways the economy of which one would perhaps have preferred. How is it to be understood? The text interprets the reader, names the inner dimensions about which one would have preferred to keep silent. How are they to be regarded? Is the reader capable of entering into interpretative dialogue with the otherness of the text? Does not one always seek somewhat to reduce otherness to the same thing? The interpretative relationship to the self in the light of the text implies a decentring of the self, since the text also speaks of the other, of this other who obliges the readers to enter into a relationship of distancing from themselves. The text interprets readers in their relationship to others, evaluates their capacity for openness to the other. Human flourishing takes place through this freedom; it is a demanding freedom, and this freedom of interpretative relationship implies a community dialogue in the relationship to the text. Doing christology consequently becomes a matter of grasping its limits, grasping its fragmented Christian identity, and not turning in on a Christian identity external to oneself, to which one can only conform externally. The flourishing of the human and the maturity of the Christian require freedom to risk oneself in a word which constructs the identity of the interpreting subject.

Transition from Christian identity to the identity of the Christian

What will be the conditions of narrative identity within theological work? Theological reason breaks up any attempt to imprison the narrative identity within subjectivity. The interpretation of the identity of the Christian involves the suspension of an *a priori* knowledge towards an open story from an action still to come, the action becoming the criteria for validating statements about the self: the other who defines himself as a Christian and the other who does not define himself as a Christian are then at the heart of the action. The ethical dimension of narrative identity thus takes place in this action, which implies a relation to other subjects in whom it is necessary to recognize the same involvement in a quest for identity. To make this a criterion of speaking is to put one's foot in the door of an identity which could be tempted to fold in on itself. The narrative which constructs a personal identity, 'thanks to the narrative coherence of events which give meaning to a biography',[3] is involved in the interaction with the stories of others.

But how can one achieve the co-existence of different stories, all of which are equally legitimate? How is it possible to respect the demand for openness to otherness, to build a community? These questions are not special to Christianity, since they run through our societies, which today are trying to rethink the nature of the 'social contract' out of respect for the demands of minorities.[4] The narrative statement must therefore issue in an interactive statement, a statement anchored in the relationship to the other. The story must make itself interpretation and argumentation, discussion and justification. The account cannot be restricted to a statement centred on itself, since more than ever the modes of social relationships in the contemporary world are formed by the demands of dialogue in the public arena. The narrative identity is called on to construct itself by exposing the modalities of its act of interpretation in an argumentative act which reconstructs its relationship to itself and the other. The process involves the narration, interpretation, justification and reconstruction of a saying presented as an action: the construction of meaning issues in a statement which is not an abstract 'word' but a social act. The narration becomes 'giving an account'; it becomes an act of constructing community life in speech action responsible for presenting in one way or another the conditions of its word.

Theological reflection today constitutes a privileged instance of the differentiation of the conditions of talking about identity in the church. Believing discourse has the duty to 'give an account of its hope' (I Peter 3.15), and this is an opportunity for theological work today to become multiform by rooting itself in quests for identities which are at the crossroads: feminist theologies, black theologies, theologies of liberation are certainly founded on accounts of identity which are primarily of a narrative order, but their mode of elocution is structured on the shock of othernesses. The different forms taken by believing discourse bring about this relationship to the construction of meaning, which presents action as a form of validating the different forms of speaking. The ethical element of narrative identity has its place precisely in this opening to argumentative identity: the construction of the narrative coherence of the events of one's life can no longer ignore the element of giving an account of one's identity to the other.

From speaking to action, the validation of the statement of belief by the community relates more to the act of putting itself in the space of dialogue and to the capacity to give an account of the conditions for this statement, rather than to its actual content. 'My identity as individual subject does not necessarily depend on an anticipated universal recognition of the truth or correctness of the attempt that I make', but rather on 'the recognition by others of my capacity to enter into the discussion with regard to the validity of what I say'.[5] Thus it is the ethical element of the speaking by the subject who is the reader that makes all the difference; it is the way in which the reading is done that leads towards the argumentation and reconstruction in discussion which aims at the construction of meaning.

The interpretation and argumentation of the other prove indispensable in breaking out of imprisonment in a narrative which legitimates itself, in an account which revolves only around an aesthetic of the self. A narrative identity which cannot encounter the word of the other can only be jeopardized by its non-recognition of the other: what good is a story without an interlocutor? It is a bottle thrown into the sea waiting for the other, the recognition of the other, the regard of the other. So the identity of the Christian does not imply being closed in on oneself; it is rather a quest for the ethical instance of the encounter with the other.

Conclusion

Meaning is not given once for all, needing only to be received or be appropriated, to be integrated into a structure of identity. Following Jesus Christ is not channelled in a way that has already been traced out. On the contrary, the suspension of meaning implies that the transition from narrative identity to argumentative identity which gives place to the identity of the Christian continually has to be remade in relation to ever different contexts. In fact the story of the dialogue with the other has not yet been written, nor have the conditions for its realization. Reading and interpreting the scripture implies following a course within which a meaning presents itself only *a posteriori*. Just as the interpretation of the identity of Jesus is a process which has continually to be taken up again, from generation to generation, without a fixed content outside the work of the interpreter, but inserted into a meaning already present that still has to state itself to us, similarly the interpretation of our narrative and argumentative identities cannot be based on fixed contents. Were that the case, what would become of freedom if the roads were paved before we traced the course of our stories on them?

The work *on* the reader of the text and the work *in* the reader and *of* the reader each time produce an original story. The reader interprets, and after interpreting must continually resume interpretation in the breaches opened up by the suspension of meaning. Meaning waits for us to 'go over the traces of faith again',[6] to leave these fresh traces, still warm, for those who follow us, to make a sign in our turn to future generations, to open up space for interpretation to them so that they also take risks in their turn: 'to attest that the word has touched us so that others involve themselves in the risk of reading'.[7] That is to be called a living tradition.

Such a theory of interpretation takes place in a theological reason which primarily will not be individual, since it includes a concern for social criticism, the criticism of ideologies, and since it aims at making others enter into a movement of 'conversion'. Narrative identity and argumentative identity are to be reconciled in the identity of a Christian which is not defined by a content but by its manner towards the other.

Christology can be constructed in many ways, but the challenge consists in finding how the maturity of the Christian is taken account of. In all theological and christological discourse, the epistemological demand of our age requires us to evaluate the conditions for the realization of the human.

What is the aim of interpretation? It is to discover oneself interpreted in the movement of the act of reading and to discover oneself in a relation of otherness, in both directions.

Notes

1. Curiously, in a Gospel which has otherwise been characterized by the 'secret' surrounding his identity.

2. Cf. my 'Du sens à la signification: pour une théorie de l'acte de lecture en théologie', *Laval théologique et philosophique* 52/2, June 1996, 327–38.

3. Jean-Marc Ferry, 'Sur la responsabilité à l'égard du passé. L'éthique de la discussion comme éthique de la rédemption', *Hermes* 10, 1991, 133; id., 'La question

de la religion. De l'identité narrative à l'identité reconstructive', in *L'individu, le citoyen, le croyant*, Brussels 1993, 91–9.

4. Charles Taylor, *Multiculturalism and 'the Politics of Recognition'*, Princeton 1992.

5. Jürgen Habermas, *La pensée postmetaphysique. Essais philosophiques*, Paris 1993, 187–241.

6. I have taken this expression from Louis Panier, *La naissance du fils de Dieu. Sémiotique et théologie discursive. Lecture de Luc 1–2*, Paris 1991. This book suggests going beyond a 'definition of divine identity for Jesus' towards an approach which allows us to hear something 'of our own humanity and the place where God encounters us as human beings, since we are first of all sons' (7).

7. Jean Calloud, 'Le texte à lire', in *Le temps de la lecture. Exégèse biblique et sémiotique*, Paris 1993, 62.

Kingdom of God, Justification and Salvation

René Kieffer

The author of the *Epistle to Diognetus* writes in the second century: 'What the soul is in the body, that the Christians are in the world. The soul is spread through all members of the body, and Christians throughout the cities of the world. The soul dwells in the body but is not of the body, and Christians dwell in the world, but are not of the world' (6.1–3).

Today Christians probably find it difficult to express so neatly their own purpose in the chaotic world in which they live. So many subtleties attach them to this earth, with which they feel in solidarity. The complexity of human, national and international relations prevents them from defining their place in the world with the simplicity to which the author of the epistle bears witness. Today more than ever our perception of ourselves is marred by all that we learn every day about the lamentable state of humanity. We cannot detach ourselves from our very daily lives, filled with trivial and ephemeral cares.

When we read the foundational texts of our faith, the suspicion arises, 'Aren't these fine words so many lures to tempt us?'. Christians have become disunited in the name of justification by faith; they have been persecuted in order to establish their true understanding of eternal life; they have scorned social realities to promote their own conception of the kingdom of God and the new creation; they have ignored the wretched fate of their neighbour to assure their own salvation in a narcissistic way. Our memory is mutilated by all the abuses to which the fanatical use of the Bible has led (and continues to lead). How do we rediscover a 'second naiveté' after our multiple suspicions of a language which seems to have seduced Christians too much?

Here I propose to clear a way through some of the minefields of Holy

Scripture. I want to demonstrate the very human presuppositions on which the Christian revelation takes place in the Bible. Starting from the canonical Gospels, we shall be considering the notions of the kingdom of God and eternal life. Above all with the help of Paul and John I shall try to illuminate the profound meaning of justification, salvation and the new creation. My exposition will be limited, but it aims to bring out something which, though in a language which is difficult to understand today, continues to have value for the personal orientation of the Christian.

I Kingdom of God and eternal life in the Gospels

Greek has only one word, *basileia*, to express notions which are denoted by three different words in English: royalty, reign and kingdom. *Basileia* means 'kingdom' in the Beatitudes of Matt. 5.3, 10; 'royalty' in the scene in which Jesus appears before Pilate in John 18.36; and 'reign' in most of the Gospel texts. In the Old Testament, concrete royalty or kingship and the ideology which surrounds it are interpreted in an eschatological perspective in the prophets and the apocalyptic literature. Kingship came to be the vehicle of the expectation of a messianic era in which right and justice would be finally realized (see e.g. Ps. 72). The experience of oppression under foreign kings led the Jewish people to hope that one day God would replace all those who oppressed them. As the prophet says, 'And in the days of those kings the God of heaven will set up a kingdom which shall never be destroyed, nor shall its sovereignty be left to another people. It shall break in pieces all these kingdoms and bring them to an end, and it shall stand for ever' (Dan. 2.44).

In the time of Jesus it was thought that the kingdom of God, with its saving power, remained hidden, since the pagans continued to oppress Israel. In the Kaddish, a very ancient prayer to which Jesus refers in the 'Our Father', pious Jews expressed this as follows: 'May the great name of God be magnified and sanctified in the world which he has created according to his will. May he soon establish his kingdom, in your life and your days, and in the life of the house of Israel.'

It is this future reign that Jesus proclaims in our canonical Gospels. As Mark wrote: 'There are those standing here who will not taste of death before they see the kingdom of God come with power' (Mark 9.1; cf. Matt. 16.28; Luke 9.27). For the evangelists, this power has been prefigured in the transfiguration and manifested in the resurrection, but it awaits the coming of Christ for its final fulfilment. This chronological ambiguity is also present in the proclamation of Jesus: 'The time is fulfilled and the kingdom of God is at hand' (Mark 1.15; see Matt. 4.17). A similar form appears in the source common to Matthew and Luke (Matt. 10.5–7 and Luke 9.2; Matt. 12.28; Luke 11.20). What does it mean? Do we have to emphasize the use of the perfect *eggiken* and say that the kingdom of God has already arrived, referring to the *epthasen* in Matt. 12.28 and Luke 11.20? Or do we have to understand that the kingdom of God has come close, the more normal meaning of *eggiken*? The discussion of this question has been intense among a great many exegetes.[1] In any case, the question cannot be settled solely on the basis of the use of the two verbs. At most one can say that the time of fulfilment has come.

For our evangelists, Jesus is aware of the proximity of the last time. He invites all those who hear him to be converted and to believe in the Good News which he proclaims. Radical decisions need to be taken by those who want to enter the kingdom of God, since it is 'better to enter the kingdom of God with one eye than with two eyes to be thrown into Gehenna' (Mark 9.47). Jesus himself expects one day to be able to participate in the messianic feast in the kingdom of God (Mark 14.25), which is already prefigured in the miracle of the multiplication for the Jews (Mark 6.32–44), and in the bread for the Gentiles (Mark 7.24–30).

With the help of parables which remain paradoxical, the mysterious character of the growth of the kingdom of God is announced. At the moment of the preaching of Jesus, this kingdom has only begun. The seed is sown and bears fruit if it falls on good ground (Mark 4.3–20 par.). The reader is implicitly invited to be good ground for this seed, which needs solid roots. The kingdom of God grows like the seed, which grows of its own accord until the day of the harvest (Mark 4.26–29). The grain of mustard seed can seem to be the smallest seed in the world, but when it is sown it becomes far greater than any shrub (Mark 4.30–32 par.).

In one sense the kingdom of God has already come in the person of Jesus. It is manifest in all the miracles that he performs to confirm his proclamation of the Good News. The Twelve serve as models for all believers called in their turn to listen to the Master. But despite the manifestations of the power of Jesus, the disciples remain hardened and are not yet open to the revelation of their Master's secret (cf. Mark 6.52; 8.17). The initiation into the glory of the transfigured Christ prepares the three main disciples, Peter, James and John (Mark 9.2ff. par.), to understand the sense in which Jesus will be raised.

Matthew and Luke present a much more complex view of the teaching of Jesus, with all its moral and spiritual demands, but they maintain Mark's principal perspective on the question of the kingdom of God. By contrast,

John reinterprets the kingdom of God and sees it made concrete in the person of Jesus, who gives life to the believer. Hence the announcement of the kingdom is identical with the proclamation of the work of God which Jesus has come to accomplish on the part of his Father. Since C. H. Dodd[2] commentators have liked to talk of a realized eschatology in connection with the Fourth Gospel. The judgment has already taken place on this earth: 'He who believes in him is not judged; he who does not believe is judged already' (John 3.18). Faith also makes it possible to live eternal life in the present: 'So must the Son of man be lifted up, that whoever believes in him may have eternal life' (John 3.15; see 3.36; 6.40, 47).

The Fourth Gospel and the Synoptic Gospels supplement one another: in Mark, Matthew and Luke the kingdom of God is like a code which allows believers to interpret their lives here on earth in a dynamic perspective of development. A spiritual and moral struggle makes the seed of the kingdom grow among human men and women, but its fulfilment will come only in the last time, which for every man and every woman coincides with the limit imposed on them by personal death. By contrast, John invites the believer to live the mystery of the life and love of God in the present. This presence gives the necessary power and distance for any struggle for the kingdom of God.

II Justification, salvation and new creation in Paul and John

(*a*) Confronted with the abuse of works of piety in this time, Martin Luther was right to protest and to restore to justification by faith its full weight in the understanding of the Christian message. In fact there was a risk that Paul's important discovery would be forgotten. But Luther was wrong to project his own anguish and his struggles against the papacy on to the Pauline texts.

It is always interesting to re-read the three commentaries which he devoted to the first explicit statement of Paul on justification, the conflict between Peter and Paul in Antioch related in Gal. 2.11–21.[3] We can see that here Luther made a discovery which completely transformed his life. As a monk he tried to gain the approval of a strict God who reflected the features of his physical father. He suddenly discovered that God was above all a God of mercy who invites all to live by the grace of Christ.

As the apostle to the Gentile recalls, the works of the law did not justify either Peter or himself, but only faith in Jesus Christ (Gal. 2.16). In re-establishing the demands of the law ('If I build up again those things which I tore down', 2.18), Peter and Paul were making themselves transgressors.

'But I (Paul, Peter and every Christian) through the law died to the law, that I might live to God' (2.19). Here Paul supposes that Christ, who died an accursed death on the cross, has paid to free us from the curse of the law (see 3.13). Moreover from now on the blessing accorded to Abraham comes down to all, Jews and Gentiles (see 3.14). It is because of this transfer brought about by Christ that Paul can write in almost mystical transports: 'I have been crucified with Christ; it is no longer I who live, but Christ who lives in me; and the life I now live I the flesh I live by faith in the Son of God, who loved me and gave himself for me' (2.19f.).

In his fictitious words addressed to Peter and the other Christians in Antioch in Gal. 2.14–21, Paul has passed from an 'I' which includes Peter, Paul and all the Jewish Christians to an 'I' which describes his personal experience. Since Albert Schweitzer,[4] exegetes have discussed at length whether or not the Pauline mysticism comes before the doctrine of justification by faith. In my view, justification by faith is fundamental in Paul's mature writings and goes beyond the question of the integration of the Jews and Gentiles into the same church. The quasi-mystical experience of faith in Christ dead and risen led Paul at a very early stage to emphasize the importance of the grace of God in salvation.

In the letter to the Romans the apostle ended by developing his thesis of justification by faith in all its breadth. To establish it he went beyond the pessimism of numerous Jews who accepted that all just men on occasion committed sins. He emphasizes that the Jews with their law are no more advanced than the pagans, since all can be called 'sinners'.[5] In Gal. 2.15 Paul as a Jew could still characterize the Gentiles as 'sinners'. But now he emphasizes that even the Jews must be considered sinners: 'For there is no distinction; since all have sinned and fall short of the glory of God, they are justified by his grace as a gift, through the redemption which is in Christ Jesus' (Rom. 3.23f.). He can also write: 'While we were yet sinners Christ died for us . . . For as by one man's disobedience many were made sinners, so by one man's obedience many will be made righteous' (Rom. 5.18, 19).

It is this aspect which Luther brings out in his commentaries, which has led to justification by faith being considered in the Protestant tradition an *articulus stantis et cadentis ecclesiae*, an article by which the church stands or falls.[6] Because of Luther's opposition to monastic practices, there have been misunderstandings. Paul always thought that faith produced fruits (Phil. 1.11; Rom. 7.4) and even a good work (Phil. 1.6; II Cor. 9.8), but he fought against those who thought that the works of the law could lead to faith in Christ. Already as a Jew he knew that Christ had all the initiative in the election of Israel and in his covenant with him. But 'the words of the law' encouraged by Jewish practice could block faith in the dead and risen Christ because, according to the fine saying of Thérèse of Lisieux, for those who are profoundly religious, 'all is grace'.

We can also note that in the Fourth Gospel. Faith in Jesus gives us access to eternal life. Like Paul, the evangelist knows that this faith is a free gift of God. Jesus comes from the Father and performs his work according to God's commandment (John 10.18; 12.49f.; 14.31; 15.10). He glorifies his Father on earth and his Father in turn confers on him on the cross the glory which he had from the beginning (see 17.1–5). It is the Father who has put all into the hands of the Son (3.35). This power conferred on Jesus is subsequently identified by his subsequent possibilities: to judge (5.22, 27), to possess life in himself (5.26), to say words which come from the Father (12.49; 17.8), to receive the name and the glory of the Father (17.11f., 22), and finally to have authority over all flesh (17.2). It is also the Father who gives disciples to Jesus (6.37; 17.6) and who loves them (17.23, 26). So every initiative comes from the Father, including that of being able to believe in Jesus: 'The work of God is to believe in the one whom he has sent' (6.29). Just as Jesus reflects the initiative of the Father in all things, it is again God who acts in all that he does for his disciples.

In its roots in the Old Testament, justification is not centred on individual salvation, but has cosmic elements. Just as the Egyptian notion of truth (ma'at) expresses the harmony which reigns between the universe and society, so justice (zedeq) in the Old Testament describes just relations between human beings and God. It is God who is just and justifies Israel by his covenant and the Torah, which is less a 'law' than continual teaching. It is in this sense that for Paul Abraham becomes a model of justice by his faith. It is necessary to go back beyond the covenant on Sinai to the promises given to Abraham, the father of believers.

(b) Paul and John use different vocabularies, but they meet up when they describe their experience of divine initiatives. We can also confirm that in their presentation of salvation and the new creation.

The title 'Saviour' is not much used in the Gospels, but features more in the late writings of the New Testament. Paul uses it once in a clearly eschatological context: 'Our commonwealth is in heaven, and from it we await a saviour, the Lord Jesus Christ' (Phil. 3.20).

Despite this eschatological orientation of the title in Paul, in the Gospels the role of saviour is fully assumed by Jesus in his earthly activity, his death and his resurrection. In performing his therapeutic miracles Jesus in a sense serves all those who need him. In these miracles salvation consists in regaining health and even life, but that does not change the mortal condition of human beings in any way. The Gospels presuppose a more definitive salvation, which consists in conquering death itself. When Jesus forgives the sins of a sick man, he signifies that his activity in proclaiming the kingdom of God also relates to eternal life. His life, his death and his resurrection reorientate the fate of human beings on a state of life in which death is definitely conquered.

John expresses that more clearly than the three other evangelists. Jesus' way towards Calvary and the cross is a way to the Father (see John 13.1–4). Jesus, who is thirsty and drinks vinegar, can say, 'It is fulfilled' (19.28–30), since he has truly come to accomplish the mission which has been entrusted to him by the Father. In this sense 'he is truly the saviour of the world' (4.42). For 'God did not send his son into the world to judge the world, but that the world might be saved by him' (3.17). In the Jewish tradition it is God who will raise the dead. But John does not hesitate to attribute this function to Christ: 'The hour is coming when all who are in the tombs will hear his voice and come forth, those who have done good, to the resurrection of life' (5.28f.).

What John only sketches out here, stands at the centre of Paul's thought. With a pronounced originality as compared with the Judaism around him, Paul thinks that there cannot be any resurrection outside the sphere of the risen Christ.[7] In the Old Testament eternal life in the other world remains vague. A diminished existence awaits man in Sheol. Even when the resurrection is envisaged, it seems above all to be a new earthly life, e.g. in Ezek. 37 and Dan. 12. However, we can also guess the mysterious action of God who brings up the righteous from Sheol to have them participate in his kingdom in a transfigured life (see Dan. 12.2f.). The God who has created human beings can also raise the martyrs of faith (II Macc. 7.9ff.).

These beginnings of a hope in a world beyond with God become firmer in Paul thanks to the concrete resurrection of Christ. Just as the Father has raised Jesus, so he will raise the dead in connection with the Son and his Spirit: 'That I may know him and the power of his resurrection, and may share his sufferings, becoming like him in his death, that if possible I may attain the resurrection of the dead' (Phil. 3.10f.). The reason for this is that 'Christ is risen for the dead, the first fruits of those who sleep . . . As in Adam all die, so in Christ all shall be made alive' (I Cor. 15.20). The Spirit which in Gen. 1.3 was the principle of life in creation is also the principle in the resurrection of the dead (see already Ezek. 37), but for Paul from now on the Spirit acts in accord with the risen Christ.

The apostle does not know how this new creation in Christ will take place, but he uses the analogy of the seed: 'And what you sow is not the body which is to be but a bare kernel, perhaps of wheat or of some other grain. But God gives it a body as he has chosen, and to each kind of seed its own body' (I Cor. 15.38). This image allows him to affirm a continuity despite the difference between our present body and the risen body. For Paul, the same creative power of God is at work as that which is manifested in the resurrection of Christ. The letter to the Colossians will develop this aspect and show how all is created in Christ, the firstborn among the dead (Col. 1.15–20).

A theology of creation which, beyond the fate reserved for human beings, envisages the concrete consequences of belief in the incarnation and the resurrection of the Son of God for the whole universe has to develop here a hermeneutic which takes account of the world in its most material character.[8] In this sense Paul dares to write: 'The creation waits with eager longing for the revealing of the sons of God; for the creation was subjected to futility, not of its own will but by the will of him who subjected it in hope; because the creation itself will be set free from its bondage to decay and obtain the glorious liberty of the children of God. We know that the whole creation has been groaning in travail together until now' (Rom. 8.19–22). This affirmation of faith has a place at a different level from that of a philosophical reflection on the fate of the cosmos, but is not unconnected with it. Christian salvation is not without cosmic consonances; there is 'a new earth and a new heaven'. Only then will what Paul envisages be realized: 'When all things are subjected to him, then the Son himself will also be subjected to him who puts all things under him, that God may be all in all' (I Cor. 15.28). The language of faith which describes a world of salvation and a world beyond our earthly life necessarily remains imprecise. John and Paul are not taken in by the images that they use: what interests them is to establish a living contact between the believers they address and the Christ whom they have encountered in their own lives.

Conclusion

Can such teaching still inspire Christians today? Yes, provided that they themselves have a personal experience of an encounter with Christ in their life. Perhaps more than ever the believer is called on to decipher the interventions of God in this world which seems able to pass God by.

In his classic *Old Testament Theology*,[9] Gerhard von Rad centres his account on the history of salvation. Many perspectives are drawn from the present, past and future of Israel. Von Rad uses above all the historical and prophetic books, but has difficulty in integrating the wisdom literature into his synthesis. However, his perspective of a saving plan of God remains fundamental for understanding the link between the Old and the New Testament, regardless of how real history is to be reconciled with related history.

The Jews understood the Old Testament (which they called Tanakh) in a different way by putting at the centre their own conception of the Torah, God's teaching, with its multiple haggadic and halakhic interpretations in the Mishnah and Talmud. These interpretations are thought to illuminate the way taken by the believing Jew in this life.

The Christian can derive an analogous teaching from the Bible, since according to Paul and John, Jesus brought the law to its fulfilment. Like their Jewish brothers and sisters, Christians believe that God intervenes in this world, but for them salvation has become concrete in the person of Jesus Christ. In their eyes, kingdom of God, justification, eternal life, salvation and new creation are marked with the indelible seal of the incarnation and resurrection of the Son of God.

A personal question is put to us. In a world in which violence and injustice abound, what are we to do so that this fine theology of creation and salvation are not just pious words but an inspiration for all our daily life? Conversely, if we take our faith seriously, how can we avoid being fanatics who can no longer communicate with those who do not share our hope? I think that in the face of the mass of religious opinions and convictions of which we are increasingly aware today, as Christians we should fight all isolationism and work energetically, with all men and women of good will, to improve this world which 'has been groaning in travail together until now'. The Christian faith teaches us that in the midst of the difficult questions which preoccupy all humankind we need to receive with gratitude the share of grace that has been given us. We are called to make this grace fertile in profound respect for all those men and women with whom the Son of God identified himself when he became man.

Notes

1. See the documentation in J. Carmignac, *Le Mirage de l'Eschatologie. Règne et Royaume de Dieu . . . sans Eschatologie*, Paris 1979.

2. C. H. Dodd, *The Interpretation of the Fourth Gospel*, Cambridge 1953; cf. R. Bultmann, *Theology of the New Testament* 2, London and New York 1955.

3. For more details see my *Foi et justification à Antioche. Interprétation d'un conflit (Ga 2, 14–21)*, Paris 1982.

4. A. Schweitzer, *The Mysticism of the Apostle Paul*, London 1931; see also E. P. Sanders, *Paul and Palestinian Judaism. A Comparison of Patterns of Religion*, London and Philadelphia 1977.

5. For all these questions see M. Winninge, *Sinners and the Righteous. A Comparative Study of the Psalms of Solomon and Paul's Letters*, Stockholm 1955.

6. See for example, I. Lönning, 'Paulus und Petrus. Gal. 2.11ff. als kontroverstheologisches Fundamentalproblem', *Studia Theologica* 24, 1970, 1–69.

7. I have developed this aspect in an article 'Résurrection du Christ et résurrection générale. Essai de structuration de la pensée paulinienne', *Nouvelle Revue Théologique* 103, 1981, 330–44.

8. See the eschatological cosmology of Karl Rahner, presented in P. Geister, *Aufhebung zur Eigentlichkeit. Zur problematik kosmologischer Echatologie in der Theologie Karl Rahners*, Uppsala 1996.

9. G. von Rad, *Old Testament Theology* (2 vols), London 1975.

Participation and Testimony: The Meaning of Death and Life in Jesus Christ Today

Edmund Arens

Anyone asking about the meaning of Jesus's passion, death and resurrection for the practice of Christian faith today finds an answer in Paul which is as striking as it is mysterious for men and women at the end of the twentieth century. Those texts which at the beginning of this century the History of Religions school regarded as the core of Paul's 'Christ mysticism' emphatically speak of a dying with Christ as well as a life in Jesus Christ. Here I shall sketch out what such christological discourse, which is concentrated in the letter to the Romans, means in respect of a relationship to Christ today and a spirituality and practice which is orientated on it.

To begin with I shall elucidate what Paul means by 'dying with Christ' with reference to the beginning of Romans 6. This is identified as ritual initiation which takes place in baptism. Then I shall discuss 'living in Christ' as interactive communion in connection with Romans 8. Finally I shall demonstrate the practical implications and consequences of death and life in Jesus Christ. I shall do this under the key phrase 'bear witness to Christ'; here I shall present the dimensions of discipleship of Christ.

I Dying with Christ in ritual initiation

In connection with the representation of the death and resurrection of Jesus, Pauline theology first of all points to baptism, which stands right at the beginning of the genesis of faith; Romans 6 understands this as being crucified, dying and being buried with Jesus. For Paul, baptism in the name of Jesus at the same time means 'baptism into death' (Rom. 6.4). Because in baptism we have died 'with Christ' (Rom. 6.6), we believe that we shall also live with him. In my view four elements can be identified in the Pauline theology of baptism which is articulated here; these come together in the representation of the event of the passion. Baptism takes place in a ritual event which first represents a rite of passage. Secondly, this can be understood more precisely as a rite of initiation. Thirdly, it is ritual participation, which constitutes an inter-subjective relationship. Fourthly, this event at the same time has ethical and practical implications and consequences.

From the perspective of the sociology of religion, baptism in the name or the death of Jesus is to be understood as a rite of passage,[1] i.e. as a ritual practice which sets someone aside from a status which is given socially, locally, generationally and so on. It thus breaks off previous relations and circumstances and gives the subject of the ritual a new status through the ritual process. In my view the ritual dimension is already brought out by the comparison with being buried; here at the same time it is made clear that for the subject of the ritual this is a matter of passive acceptance, a passion to which the subject is exposed and which the subject allows to happen. Paul specifically says that the passion of Jesus is echoed in this passivity of being baptized. With the crucified Christ the person being baptized parts company with the 'old man' (Rom. 8.6), breaks the previous bonds to the powers of sin and death, and puts an end to the conditions which have previously been dominant, in order through this action to go over with Christ to a new place and enter into new relationships.

As an 'acceptance of his action and participation in his fate',[2] baptism in the name and death of Jesus is, secondly, to be regarded as a rite of initiation which introduces and integrates into a new community those who are being baptized and have detached themselves from their own ties and died to them.[3] This more general theoretical statement about ritual can be made more precise in Paul with reference to christology: baptism means following the way of Jesus and taking part in the community of the risen Christ, to whom the person baptized has been made like. Initiated into his 'saving communion',[4] those baptized attain a permanent bond with him in an intersubjective relationship which at the same time opens up the future and contains hope for eschatological participation in his resurrection.

A third aspect of baptism characterizes it as a ritual representation of what Jesus has done previously. It comprises acceptance into a new intersubjectivity, namely the community of destiny with Jesus, and thus at the same time entry into the communion of life with him in the community of his brothers and sisters (Rom. 8.29), which transcends their ritual representation and is realized in a new reciprocity, namely in the mutuality of the interactive communion 'in Christ'.

Finally, as a fourth element, baptism as being crucified with and dying with Jesus also contains an ethical practical dimension which transcends the interactive communion. This is addressed by Paul in his invitation to live as 'new men' (Rom. 6.4) and developed in the imperative in Rom. 6.12–14, where the implications and consequences of the 'transition into a new lordship'[5] which has taken place in baptism is demonstrated. The ethical-practical or christo-practical dimension of baptism entails the obligation to put into practice the liberation from enslaving sins and the powers of death which has taken place in the liberating praxis of righteousness.

II Living in Christ in interactive communion

Anyone who has died in baptism with Christ and has been buried with him already participates in some respect in his resurrection. Paul expresses this in Rom. 8 by saying that such a person lives 'in Christ'. The 'in Christ' (Rom. 8.1, 2), which is to be understood primarily in local terms, makes the 'with Christ' more precise. Anyone who has ritually followed Christ's way of suffering with him in baptism has attained in him a new life freed from the powers of death, and participates in the living power of the crucified and risen Christ, which is realized in personal and ecclesial communion with him and thus in his community. In Paul, 'in Christ' is 'an abbreviation for the theologoumenon of the body of Christ'.[6] Here the incorporation of the individual Christian and the community is addressed in a life-giving field of relationships. Both individuals and community become the sphere of the life and activity of Jesus on the basis of the saving *communio Christi* in their interactive communion with him and among one another. As members of the body of Christ they belong to him and become his members, participators and heirs. Thus their whole existence is 'defined' in a new way (Rom. 8.5), orientated on a life which accords with the Spirit of Christ and doing God's righteousness.

According to Paul, anyone who lives in Christ lives in a new reciprocity: the 'in Christ' (Rom. 8.2) is matched by the 'Christ in you' (Rom. 8.10). This mutuality can be expressed elsewhere in categories of lordship ('in the Lord'); here the lordship which frees from the slavery of sin makes possible and grants a new mutuality and is an aid towards the reciprocity of the 'children of God' (Rom. 8.16). Connected with this at the same time is an enabling to a new life in the field of a relationship with Jesus Christ and his power (cf. Gal. 2.20).

In Paul's conception, the mutuality and reciprocity of life 'in Christ' is brought to bear above all in the *ekklesia* as *koinonia*. According to Paul, *koinonia* with Jesus Christ (I Cor. 1.9) is first of all shared participation in the body of Christ, from which *koinonia* in the body of Christ proceeds (I Cor. 10.16f.). As the 'community of the Spirit' (II Cor. 13.13) of Jesus Christ it aims at an all-embracing community and is realized in the *koinonia* that the apostle has with his communities, the members of the communities have among one another and the communities have with one another, through 'mutual giving and receiving'[7] of their spiritual and material goods. The common 'being in Christ' is made concrete in the communicative interaction of the members of the communication community which is the church;[8] it is concentrated symbolically in the communicative praxis of the sacraments.[9] Such communicative praxis essentially means the communicating and sharing communication of Christ. Again it has an elementary ritual dimension in the sharing of bread and wine; however, in addition to this it calls for and embraces practical sharing of the common life in spiritual and material solidarity and responsibility for one another in the communion of the brothers and sisters of Christ.

As fellowship in and with Jesus Christ, *koinonia* as understood in the New Testament has a christological basis and – in the Synoptic Gospels more clearly than in Paul – is grounded in the communicative praxis of Jesus. As the communion of those who participate in him and through him have become together the body of Christ, at the same time it has a practical orientation. As 'fellowship in his suffering' (Phil. 3.10), it includes an element of suffering. Moreover it has an ecclesial dimension, in so far as it defines the relationship of fellowships within communities and the links between communities in reciprocal responsibility and care.

But the 'in Christ' not only genetically presupposes the 'with him' but also necessarily entails it. Only that person is in Christ 'who is with Christ, who follows his way and accepts "the common destiny of the follower with the initiator"'.[10] To become a 'fellow heir with Christ' (Rom. 8.17), one needs to share not only in his saving community but at the same time in his way which leads to suffering. The *communio Christi* is essentially the *koinonia* of the crucified Christ, fellowship in the broken and divided body, and therefore a *communio passionis*.

The ritual dying and being buried with Christ and the communicative life of *communio* in the *koinonia* of Jesus Christ which is intensified ritually and liturgically in the fellowship of the eucharistic meal[11] is accordingly a stimulus to share this with others, so that it is shared in the fellowship of the children of God. Such sharing, which is aimed at others becoming partakers, is one of the elementary goals of christopraxis, both individual and collective.[12]

III Bearing witness to Christ in the christopraxis of discipleship

Anyone who has been crucified and buried with Christ, and as a result has been 'made like to' him (Rom. 6.5) and has 'put him on' as a garment (Gal. 3.27), is also to 'walk according to his Spirit' (Rom. 8.5). Every Christian is called and enabled to bear witness to him (I Cor. 1.6). Participation and testimony are consequently related. Participation in the death and life of Jesus are actualized in 'participation in the *martyria Jesu*'.[13] The life 'in Christ' which is based on dying 'with Christ' is accomplished in the christopraxis of discipleship. Therefore it is important to bear comprehensive witness to Christ beyond the ritual and liturgical communication of Christ and the fellowship of communion in and with him.

In my view, this happens in the fourfold way of kerygmatic-missionary witnessing, diaconal witnessing, prophetic witnessing and the witnessing of suffering.[14] Kerygmatic-missionary testimony communicates the gospel of Jesus Christ for the purpose of its being shared. Kerygmatic-missionary witnessing expresses the gospel in its christopraxis and by that communicates what is witnessed to those who are being addressed. To this degree Christian witness is essentially missionary. That applies even when the predominant praxis of Christian mission and the imperialistic and Eurocentric understanding of mission which has developed are to be put in question.[15]

Kerygmatic-missionary witnesses want to convince people of Jesus Christ by their praxis. All those who take on the communication of the gospel and in their praxis make Jesus accessible and visible, acquaint others with him so as to confront them with him and invite them to be his disciples, are such witnesses. This explicit communication of the gospel has its foundation and criterion in the apostolic witness. Like that witness it attempts to bring Jesus' person and praxis, his action and that of God in and to him, near to others and seeks to bring them to participate in the praxis of Jesus which has been made visible in their own witnessing. Kerygmatic-missionary witnessing makes the core of the gospel accessible and transparent in its own witnessing, so that 'attention is directed towards

Jesus Christ in such a way that it can depict itself in its own perspective, be there for others, and thus become relevant in this context'.[16]

In being addressed to others, such witness at the same time seeks a following and calls for assent.[17] As witness to the rule and righteousness of God which has dawned with Jesus and which through his death frees for new life, it seeks to come to an understanding with those to whom it is addressed. Kerygmatic missionary witnessing perverts itself when it builds on colonializing subjection, strategic indoctrination and repressive techniques instead of inviting communicative praxis. Kerygmatic-missionary witnessing is aimed at convincing people of the person of Jesus, his communicative liberating praxis of the *basileia* and righteousness of God, and inviting them to join in this practice which is made possible by God's action, and accordingly to christopraxis.

Diaconal witnessing takes place where people turn to others to support them, to stand by them in their need and give them help. It takes place where people are in solidarity with the needy, the suffering and the oppressed and hand on solidarity with Jesus by acting in his spirit. Those who do this become diaconal witnesses to Jesus Christ. Whether in social and charitable or political diaconia,[18] they adopt Jesus' structure of action, live by his solidarity and fellowship with the poor, the disenfranchised and the weak, and point to Jesus' praxis and person in their own action.

An essential element of diaconal testimony is the help which believers give one another in complete equality and reciprocity.[19] In turning to others, standing up for them, supporting them in their distress, offering help and being in solidarity with them, they testify to a praxis which is in solidarity with Jesus. This praxis of diaconal witnessing is concerned to relieve human suffering, to free people from their distress and oppression and the injustice that is inflicted on them. Since the witness enters into relationship with those who are being addressed, diaconal witness aims at making possible and building up relationships in solidarity. Without deliberately intending it, such a praxis may prove convincing and attractive and thus convince people of Jesus' practice of universal solidarity.

Prophetic witnessing takes place where people make claims in the name of Jesus and the God of Jesus Christ against the dominant powers of sin and death, where they intervene in God's 'dispute' with the world and take his side. Such witnessing, which criticizes injustice, denounces oppressive domination and sets God's promised liberation and his liberating rule against it, is the praxis of prophetic witness. 'Witnessing includes the aspects of classical prophecy: making accusations about sinful conditions and announcing a new world.'[20] The prophetic witness sets prevailing conditions and powers before God's judgment, stands up to make accusations of injustice, and along with God's demands presents God's promise of a new and just society which is beneficial for human beings. Prophetic witnesses demonstrate this new order symbolically in their actions and anticipate it, as did Jesus in his praxis of prophetic solidarity. In so doing they prove to be agents of innovation, whose claim, protest and accusation is embedded in a new humanizing praxis. Anyone who acts prophetically bears witness to the person and practice of Jesus, who opposes all injustice, denounces any oppression and exploitation, and sets against it the liberating rule of God. Today, all those are prophetic witnesses to Jesus Christ who fight in his name against the various powers of sin and death and champion the cause of survival and a life worth living for human beings.

The witness of suffering is that christopraxis which most strikingly reflects dying and being buried with Christ. This is given where people accept persecution, imprisonment, torture and death for their faith, and by following Jesus on his way of suffering point with their suffering to his suffering, presenting him and his passion anew and making it visible. This form of witness culminates in martyrdom. The martyr is the witness *par excellence*, who completes and seals his witness to Jesus Christ in the testimony of blood.

All those today who are persecuted for the practice of their faith bear this witness of suffering. In persecution they follow Jesus and bear witness to the presence of his person, praxis and passion. With their suffering and dying, these witnesses testify that, to use Blaise Pascal's words, Jesus' passion continues, that he lies in agony to the end of the world (*Pensée* no. 553).

In the witness of suffering the witnesses' own passion points clearly to the passion of Jesus, which the suffering witnesses make their own by following in Jesus' way of suffering. In martyrdom they become like their suffering Lord, and make him visible in their own bodies. The discipleship of Jesus in suffering can be read off the texture of the tortured victim. A witness in blood is really crucified and buried with Christ and dies, as Ignatius of Antioch (Rom. 6.1) puts it, into him in order to live in him.

Here the christopraxis of discipleship deepens into the testimony given along with one's life. Here witnessing and participation come together with the utmost intensity and urgency.

Translated by John Bowden

Notes

1. Cf. A. van Gennep, *Rites de passage*, Paris 1986; V. Turner, *The Ritual Process*, New York 1989.
2. E. Käsemann, *Commentary on Romans*, London 1982, 165 (on 6.1–11).
3. Cf. van Gennep, *Rites de passage* (n. 1), ch. 6.
4. J. Werbick, *Soteriologie*, Düsseldorf 1990, 178.
5. T. Schneider, *Zeichen der Nähe Gottes. Grundriss de Sakramententheologie*, Mainz 1992, 80.
6. Kasemann, *Commentary on Romans* (n. 2), 222 (on 8.1–11).
7. J. Hainz, *Koinonia, 'Kirche' als Gemeinschaft bei Paulus*, Regensburg 1982, 110.
8. Cf. H. Zirker, 'Die Kirche als Kommunikationsgemeinschaft', in E. Arens (ed.), *Gottesrede – Glaubenspraxis*, Darmstadt 1994, 69–88; P. Granfield (ed.), *The Church and Communication*, Kansas City 1994.
9. Cf. J. Meyer on Schlochtern, *Sakrament Kirche. Wirken Gottes im Handeln der Menschen*, Freiburg, Basel and Vienna 1992; H. O. Meuffels, *Kommunikative Sakramententheologie*, Freiburg, Basel and Vienna 1995.
10. Werbick, *Soteriologie* (n. 4), the quotation comes from Käsemann, *Commentary on Romans* (n. 2), 214.
11. Cf. the remarks on liturgical 'Christoaesthetics' in J. Wohlmuth, *Jesu Weg – unser Weg. Kleine mystagogische Christologie*, Würzburg 1992.
12. For the background to this term cf. F. Herzog, *God-Walk. Liberation Shaping Dogmatics*, Maryknoll 1988; M. K. Taylor, *Remembering Esperanza. A Cultural Political Theology for North American Praxis*, Maryknoll 1990.
13. J. Ratzinger, *Eschatologie – Tod und ewiges Leben*, Regensburg [6]1990, 89.
14. For what follows see E. Arens, *Bezeugen und Bekennen. Elementare Handlungen des Glaubens*, Düsseldorf 1989; id., *Christopraxis. A Theology of Action*, Minneapolis 1995.
15. Cf. J.-P. Jossua, *The Condition of the Witness*, London 1985; G. Collet, 'Missionarisches Handeln', in Arens (ed.), *Gottesrede* (n. 8), 150–63.
16. H. P. Siller, 'Kommunikation/Öffentlichkeitsarbeit', in C. Bäumler and N. Mette (eds.), *Gemeindepraxis in Grundbegriffen*, Düsseldorf and Munich 1987, 239–57: 251.
17. K. Rahner, 'Theological Observations on the Concept of "Witness"', *Theological Investigations* XIII, London and New York 1975, 152–169: 165.
18. Cf. H. Steinkamp, *Diakonia – Kennzeichen der Gemeinde*, Freiburg 1985; id., 'Diakonisches Handeln', in Arens (ed.), *Gottesrede* (n. 8), 131–49.
19. Thus rightly Jossua, *Condition of the Witness* (n. 15), 85.
20. J. Comblin, *Das Bild des Menschen*, Biblilothek Theologie der Befreiung, Düsseldorf 1987, 37.

Jesus, Guru of Individualism – or Community's Heart?
Christian Discipleship and Prophetic Church

Mary Grey

Franco Zefirelli's film *Francis of Assisi* offered a poignant vignette of Christian community: as the richly-vested prelates of Assisi celebrate High Mass in the Duomo in pomp and splendour, the audience realize with a shock that the Cathedral is completely empty. Where are the people? They are down in the valley with Francis and Clare, together with sheep, goats and hens, in a delightfully warm inclusive liturgy which, despite its 1960s hippy-style, leaves us in no doubt that *here is authentic Christian community*. That there is a tension between empty formalism and inclusive, involving styles of worship is indisputable. The participatory styles of being church which followed the Second Vatican Council (to some extent) meant that many people found the ceremonial formalism of traditional (male, hierarchical) worship alienating. But the question is even more challenging for a secular age. If the church is experienced as alienating and corrupt, why not live out the Christian ideals – love of neighbour, forgiveness and moral decency, to which there is still a notional commitment in society – without belonging to the Christian church? Further, the argument runs, society is multi-cultural and largely secular: without the embarrassment of church membership or the legacy of Christian imperialism, we are more likely to achieve tolerance in society. Indeed, for Western Christians it might be a way of repenting from thrusting Christianity down the throats of Jew, Muslim and indigenous peoples throughout the history of Christendom! And what a relief not to have to justify the wealth of the Vatican in the face of the grinding poverty of many of Peter's obedient servants! The prophetic, iconoclastic figure of Jesus of Nazareth, our suffering brother in struggles for justice, who broke taboos in talking to women and despised groups of people – he is not our problem: but the institutional church is!

Undoubtedly this line of arguing appeals to many. There is also the powerful argument that such a crucial figure as Mahatma Gandhi took the message of the Sermon on the Mount as foundational for his policy of non-violence, neither becoming a disciple of Jesus, nor joining a church. Indeed, he was convinced that Christianity had not even been tried. Message christology is also in vogue with an assortment of groups which include feminist theologians (who see it as a solution to the maleness of Jesus); interfaith religious leaders (who see it as a solution to the unique claims of Jesus as universal saviour); and more secular figures – like the late Dag Hammarskjøld – who see the inspiration of Jesus as a way to transform political life.

Furthermore, it is clear that, for the moment, the ethos of individualism has largely won. Most human beings – in Western Europe and North America – now seem only capable of thinking of – and feeling responsible for – their own betterment, materially speaking, and for that of their immediate family circle. Aid Agencies report a drop in their revenue. Books on spirituality, for the most part, focus on our feelings and how to get in touch with them, and counselling has become a boom industry!

This tendency has grown for many reasons: in a culture where privatization encroaches daily on the fabric of public life, it is small wonder that the private following of Jesus, or the assumption of parts of his message which happen to order personal behaviour without challenging public morality or inspiring social justice, are winning the day. It is also possible to fall back on a strand of Christian tradition to support this. From time to time there has been a reaction to a form of Christianity which appeared to govern public life excessively, expressing itself for example, in the form of Moravian Pietism[2] and Quietism,[3] both of which focussed on the hidden life of prayer and the cultivation of the interior life.

This individualistic following of Jesus can also be linked with what is perceived as the failure of liberation theology in certain parts of the world, for example, in post-Sandinista Nicaragua. When the search for the God of justice through the transformation of political and social structures appears to have failed, there is an abundance of evangelistic groups to persuade the disenchanted to follow the 'inner' message of Jesus.

Yet the hierarchicalism of the institutional church is faced in other ways, for example, by the many groups who establish creative space on the periphery.[4] There are also groups of 'loosely committed Christians' who exist without formal relationship to the established church.[5] But both of these categories are committed to the notion of community as the heart of the following of Jesus. So the issue here is both whether authentic following of Jesus can happen without community and whether this community necessarily must be an identifiable form of the Christian church.[6] There are, for example, novels like that of Nikos Kazantsakis, *Christ Recrucified*, where a romanticized notion of Jesus inspires a motley crew to disassociate itself from the institutional church in a charismatic following of Jesus.[7] I argue, first, that the following of Jesus cannot be authentic without community, and secondly, that this authenticity can be destroyed if its prophetic stance is not respected.

In the beginning, the relation . . .[8]

The inescapable feature about the earthly Jesus is not only that he brought close a God whose very being is relational – which is the core of the Christian doctrine of Trinity – but that he revealed the path to healing, redemption and transformation as consisting in right and just relationship. In fact he called people out of their isolation and alienated patterns of relating into a transformed relational way of being, where just relationships were the embodiment of the dream of the Kingdom of God. As Carter Heyward put it poetically:

> In the beginning was the relation and in the relation is the power that creates the world, through us, and with us, you and I, you and we, and none of us alone.[9]

What that means in a context of individualistic ethos of the contemporary West is that Christian discipleship offers a lifestyle completely opposed to the privatized, consumerist ethic, exploitative both of the planet's resources and of groups of poor people whom it considers expendable. For Jesus revealed sin as separation:[10] not only the construction of barriers between rich and poor, and the structural deafness which refuses to let in a different truth from the dominant story, but a blocking off from the patterns which connect body and spirit, humanity and nature. It is striking that binding images are at the heart of his parables:

> To what shall I compare the Kingdom of God? It is like leaven which a woman took and hid in three measures of meal, till it was all leavened (Luke 13.20).

It is the yeast of right and just relation which is the stuff of the Kingdom of God, whereas (in my opinion) it is the yeast of Herod against which the disciples are warned, which is the yeast of separation. But it is not only yeast which is the image of the binding agent of the Kingdom. Jesus himself functions as this, for:

> Where two or three of you are gathered together in my name, there am I in the midst of them (Matt. 18.20).

What is fundamental to the understanding of the Kingdom of God is, first, that we cannot approach Jesus except within this great dream and project – since he himself situated all his teaching in this context – and, secondly, that this relational reality is only understood as a broken body which somehow incorporates the broken and persecuted peoples of the world: *A Body Broken for a Broken People* was how Francis Moloney described the core meaning of the Eucharist.[11] This is the only way we can make sense of Paul's stress on the body of Christ – Paul, who seems not to know much about, or at least does not make central, the person of the earthly Jesus. Hence the extraordinary identification of the persecuted early Christians with the body of the suffering Jesus, with and for whom they suffered. Both women and men identified with this suffering Christ. Thus Perpetua and Felicitas, with a small community of Christians in third-century Carthage, were thrown to the lions in the arena. When Felicitas, forced to give birth to her baby in prison, was taunted by the gaoler, 'If you're complaining now, what will you do when you're thrown to the wild beasts?', she answered, 'Now it is I who suffer, but then another shall be in me, since I am now suffering for him . . .'[12]

This moving story takes us to the heart of the meaning of Christian discipleship. Contemporary debates have focussed on whether the male gender of Jesus determines the question of who can represent him, and what degree of significance this has for the incarnation. Yet christologies from different parts of the world are revealing a much greater fluidity as to the gender of Jesus. Yes, Jesus was male, but he was man in such a way as to be capable of being represented as a woman. He is a relational Christ, an ecological Christ, calling diverse and suffering communities to new expressions of power-in-relationship. What the story of Felicitas tells us is that it is the identification of Christ with the suffering and broken people – and vice versa – which is the hallmark of discipleship, because this is how healing and transformative energy is generated. Yes, Jesus is mediator of relational power – but in direct relation to the messianic communities where it is generated.

For to be a saviour figure is not to be a conventional hero like Robin Hood or El Cid. If it was, then there would be no contradiction in having our privatized posters of the hero Jesus, with whom we communicate individually. Jesus is rather anti-hero, turning the hero concept on its head. He showed, rather, that redemptive power works relationally. As the earthly Jesus, he empowered people as agents in their own self-becoming (Zacchaeus, the woman with the issue of blood, the Syro-Phoenician woman): through Jesus they were able to lay claim to their own relational strengths. Even in the most desperate of circumstances there are possibilities for relating: to remain vulnerable to this possibility – and not to give way to a destructive isolation or self-absorption – is to be open to divine redemptive action. Christ – in an extraordinary openness to a diversity of relations, both teaching and being taught – showed that the roots of the healing process must be grounded in the material and social realities of the whole of life. Matter matters is the message: not for nothing does the christology developed by Mark Kline Taylor take as starting point the image of *Christus Mater*. Focussing on the material realities of poor women as mothers as an entry point to a new christology,[13] he is able to see this Christ-figure as a challenge and corrective to sexism, hetero-sexism, racism and economic poverty.

It is a process being repeated globally through the discovery of the black Christ, the many Christa figures (including the bleeding Christa of Bosnia), the Christ of Asia who is nursing mother and shaman, tree of life, as well as suffering brother. Where there is following of Christ, there is church – but not necessarily vice versa. Where there is genuine messianic community open to and claiming the mutuality to power-in-relation, the community are making this vulnerable Christ present. And the amazing new dimension to this is that, for the first time, women are acknowledged as participating in the nexus of symbols which mediate sacred power.

It comes as no surprise to learn that where these examples of discipleship and messianic communities are at their most vibrant is on the periphery, the prophetic margins, in what might be called 'creative boundary living'.[14] Yet, as long as these groups remain on the margins, their existence is tolerated. But the dilemma is that once the prophetic groups challenge the centre, the solid weight of hierarchical authority comes into play: loyalty to the centre demands submission, yet loyalty to the prophetic core seeks another more subversive solution. Is there any way out of the dilemma which is true to the prophetic nature of Christ-community yet does not reject the institutional church?

A new church, waiting to be born?

As we approach the millennium, hopes and dreams abound for the future of the church. Millennial times are times when the prophetic spirit of God is perceived as active. Indeed there are signs that a quiet revolution is under way, that the seeds of renewal which the church so desperately needs, if it is to be seen as authentic following of Jesus – as described above – are indeed at hand. Seven factors are pointing the way.

First, communal following of Christ presents a counter-cultural challenge to the ethics of individualism and competitive materialism. In this sense the social teaching of the church ecumenically, and in particular the more than a hundred years' tradition of political and social critique of the Roman Catholic magisterium, is an invaluable resource. There is no way that the individualized following of the hero Jesus (however inspirational) can have such a structural impact.

Where this communal following is now found at its most vibrant is both among poor people in the basic ecclesial communities with their powerful hunger for social justice, and in the growing evangelical groups whose emphasis is on prayer, fellowship and social action. This was recently eloquently expressed by Rodolfo Cardenal, the Jesuit Vice-Rector of the University of Central America, when he called for a culture of simplicity to enable the crucified peoples of Central America to survive.[15]

Thirdly, from the plurality of christologies now developing, as I have been showing – the accent shifts from the person of Jesus to the redeeming dynamic which he sets in motion. The contextualized needs of the community – hunger for justice, resistance to oppression, the need to come to terms with pluralism and the cherished traditions which have shaped the community[16] – all affect the shaping of an emergent christology. This diversity in understanding Jesus today, instead of giving cause for concern, should rather fuel the conviction that christology can be transformative of culture. Excessive concern for uniformity only serves to suppress the redemptive potential of christological symbolism. The burning need today is for understanding and sharing with other faith communities. Hence a further criterion for Christian discipleship will be recognized in the degree of openness to divine truth revealed across the religious traditions. Faith community engaging with faith community – this is both discipleship and a prerequisite for world peace.

Yet another pointer issues from feminist theology's reflection on the ministry of women. Whether this springs from Anglican and Free Church experience on the actual praxis of women's ministry, or from Roman

Catholic commitment (however weak!) to collaborative ministry, the force of the theological core which emerges cannot be suppressed. That women bring gifts to ministry born of commitment to mutuality, empathy and right relationship is part of this. That women seem to have a deep capacity for forgiveness for centuries of exclusion and discrimination is astonishing. But there is more to it. What Roman Catholic women are now saying with a degree of urgency is that the mere permission for the ordination of women will not solve deeply-rooted ecclesial problems: a radical re-think of discipleship and the nature of church along prophetic and non-hierarchical lines is what is urgently needed.[17] If discipleship is seen on communal/relational lines, then the community itself embodies the suffering and risen faces of Jesus – and community consists of women and men.

The fifth pointer is a counterbalance to a theology of structural sin. Sin has its structures – but grace has its structures too. Authentic following of Christ means that grace-filled encounters are enabled through the quality of community. Young people are exploring new expressions of church and active discipleship within, for example, the ambience of creation spirituality and in the global movement known as Women Church.[18] The christology inspiring these examples is, first, the ecological Christ, as the pattern which connects the whole of creation – extending the idea of community beyond the merely human; and the affirmation that women are church, and Christa community is where messianic power is nurtured and shared.[19]

The next two points are closely linked. Millennial times are the age of the Spirit – of Christ and of God. It is the role of the Spirit to discover the cracks of culture, open up new possibilities and to lead into a yet uncharted future. It can be no accident that from various Christian communities the search for prophetic leadership is becoming powerful, a leadership which is shared, which enables and empowers the gifts of others. It is no accident that the Spirit is creating a new vulnerability towards listening and acknowledging the truth of others, particularly the truth of groups on the periphery – like AIDS sufferers and the gay community. But how does the Spirit respond to culture's preference for privatized following of Jesus?

By recognizing that social action is not enough, that people also hunger to experience God in the depth of their hearts, the dimension of mysticism and contemplation is being rediscovered, not as the private possession of the élite, but as the rootedness of the entire people of God in the presence of Christ, a presence which binds, heals, connects with the life-renewing energies of the cosmos.

This expression – prophetic and mystical – of the communal discipleship of Jesus which is suggestive of a renewed church is well expressed by the inspiring words of the late Penny Lernoux, a journalist in Latin America:

The People of God will continue their march, despite the power plays and intrigue in Rome. And the Third World will continue to beckon to the west, reminding it of the Galilean vision of solidarity. As a young Guatemalan said, a few months before she was killed by the military, 'What good is life unless you give it away – unless you can give it for a better world, even if you never see that world but have only carried your grain of sand to the building site? Then you're fulfilled as a person.'[20]

Fulfilment, self-realization, yes: but only Christian if in the solidarity of prophetic community.

Notes

1. I do not mean to criticize the importance of counselling, or understanding feelings, but to point out that this is a Euro-American focus, which has damaging effects when accompanied by an indifference to 'thinking community' and inertia over global poverty. At a retreat centre recently, where I was leading a retreat with a social justice group, it was noted that the bookshop contained not a single book on social justice. And bookshops stock what people buy.

2. Continental Pietism was a movement greatly renewing Protestant church life in the seventeenth and eighteenth centuries. A reaction partly to moral lassitude, and partly to clergy control, it encouraged people to discover their own spiritual priesthood through conversion, prayerful Bible study and devotions. See Cheslyn Jones et al. (eds), *Dictionary of Spirituality*, London 1986, 448–53.

3. Quietism is a seventeenth-century movement usually associated with Mme de Guyon and Fénelon, Archbishop of Cambrai. Mme de Guyon stressed the union of the soul with God, coupled with detachment from the world (*Dictionary of Spirituality* [n. 2], 408–15).

4. Basic ecclesial communities fall into this category, as well as justice and peace groups, and the Women Church movement.

5. When Charles Davis left the priesthood in 1967 it was for this kind of option. However, I know of no group – as opposed to individuals – which has stood the test of time.

6. I think this is to pose the question at a deeper level than whether the church of Christ is found only within the Roman Catholic Church.

7. Nicos Kazantsakis, *Christ Recrucified*, London 1962. In this novel a Greek village casts roles for its passion play. The part of Jesus falls to Manolios, the shepherd boy. Remarkably, the villagers grow into their roles. When a landless band of refugees arrives, the 'institutional church' rejects them, but they are supported by Manolios and his friends. The book ends with the murder of Manolios and his friends by the 'institutional church' – at the foot of the cross.

8. Martin Buber, *I and Thou*, Edinburgh [2]1958, 18.

9. Carter Heyward. *The Redemption of God*, Washington, DC 1980, 172.

10. See M. Grey, *The Wisdom of Fools?*, London 1993, Ch. 5, 'The Separate Self and the Denial of Relation'.

11. Francis Moloney, *A Body Broken for a Broken People*, Melbourne 1990.

12. P. Wilson-Kastner, G. R. Castner et al. (eds.), 'The Martyrdom of Perpetua. A Protest Account of Early Christianity', in *A Lost Tradition: Women Writers of the Early Church*, Washington DC 1981, 27.

13. Mark Kline Taylor, *Remembering Esperanza: A Cultural and Political Theology for North American Praxis*, Maryknoll 1990.

14. See Hannah Ward and Jennifer Wild, *Guard the Chaos. Finding Meaning in Change*, London: 1995.

15. Rodolfo Cardenal SJ, 'The Crucified People', in *Reclaiming Vision: Justice, Liberation and Education*, Inaugural Summer School 1994, LSU College, Southampton, 12–18.

16. Taylor, *Remembering Esperanza* (n. 13), Ch. I, describes the need for christology to resist oppression, respond to tradition and relate to pluralism as *a postmodern trilemma*.

17. See Elizabeth Schüssler Fiorenza, *Feminist Women Priests – an Oxymoron?*, WOC lecture, November 1995.

18. Matthew Fox, *Original Blessing – A Primer in Creation Spirituality*, Santa Fé, 1981; and Rosemary Radford Ruether, *Women Church. Theology and Practice*, San Francisco 1985.

19. Cf. Rita Nakashima Brock, *Journeys by Heart: A Christology of Erotic Power*, New York 1988.

20. Penny Lernoux, cited in Jim Wallis, *Soul of Politics*, San Diego and New York 1995, 252. .

The Vision of a New *Concilium*

Dietmar Mieth

Many questions concern us on the threshold of a further reform of *Concilium*. There can be no real continuity without change. Why do we – the people who make *Concilium* – remain faithful to our project and our movement? For *Concilium* is not only an international journal appearing in many languages, but a theological and church movement: with great intellectual independence and without subventions, open to the signs of the time and the indications of new developments, combining universal problems with a regional presence, building bridges between theological theory and church practice. We want to maintain the universality of *Concilium*, a hallmark of the theological journal. Nevertheless we remain sensitive to the various developments in different regions of the world. Before we recall our common source, common criterion and common spirit, we need to look at the development of churches and theologies in the various continents.

I Continental developments[1]

1. *Africa*

The great tensions in political and social conditions partly stem from the confrontation and overlapping of different worlds. On the one hand we must note the various value and symbol systems of the different African population groups, which have an effect not only in the religious sphere but also in social ethics and politics. On the other hand, in politics and economics these systems are overlaid with Western institutional culture. The church also shares in these tensions and in this interlocking. In what strata it is at home, how it deals with tensions, what alliances it makes or rejects, all this is important and must be prepared for by theological thinking. What integration of the different worlds can be envisaged (e.g. in matters of marriage and family, in the status of men and women, or in relation to the cult of ancestors, the special culture of life and solidarity) and where conflicts are to be tolerated are important issues here. Increasingly, an African theology is being developed which pursues independently the themes with which it has been confronted and which makes it own selections from the European theologies with which it is 'overlaid'.

These tensions are to be understood not only horizontally but also vertically in the African societies. The social and economic élites are set apart from the broad mass of the population. As a result of their assimilation to 'Western' rules in business and politics (while at the same time maintaining traditional symbols as a pretext for legitimate undemocratic behaviour), these élites play a double game which is not understood by the population and into which the broad masses are not drawn. The politics of the industrial states favours these élites to an extreme degree and thus increases the underlying tensions instead of diminishing them.

In its new sphere 'Global Perspectives', *Concilium* will increasingly tackle such questions and confidently attempt to overcome the logistic difficulties of literary collaboration with African theologians.

2. Latin America

Here, too, many people are excluded from any economic activity and a few earn a great deal. For example in Brazil ten per cent of the population earn more than sixty per cent of the national income. In many countries the situation is no better, and in some it is worse. The policy of the international institutions, e.g. CEPAL, to develop a strategy orientated on poverty for internal security so far has envisaged no more comprehensive structural changes.

For the first time in its history, Latin America is experiencing a tidal wave of secularization which is not just reaching the thin layer of the upper classes, as happened in the wake of the Enlightenment. This wave is reinforced by the growing presence of the mass media in wide layers of the population (a new opium of the people). In the cold climate of secular culture, often abandoned by fossilized church institutions, people are looking for new warmth, for an atmosphere of security and help in manageable groups. One consequence of this is the strong formation of mostly free-church sects. Their power of attraction is to be explained from their promise to work on the way in which people have been traumatized by their social marginalization. Many of these sects have the character of self-help groups, in which such experiences are integrated. Usually Christian base communities cannot profit from this situation because they usually seek to involve (intact) families. Although they do not focus directly on the traumatized individuals, the sects are especially concerned with them and their needs. Behind the sects are often quite different economic forces from those which favour the base communities over church institutions.

A new growing self-awareness of the Indios and African groups can be noted. They have come also to influence the city milieu, and are developing indigenous elements. In detaching itself from the cultural patterns of the Spanish and Portuguese colonial period, Latin America is engaged in a process of cultural pluralization which is also having an effect on the church. This includes a variety of syncretisms. How can regional churches and theologies show their perspective here? Liberation theology is threatening to lose its significance. That is not just because of the limitations put on it by the official church but also because of the way in which institutions (ecclesiastical, political, and economic) have taken over its key terms ('liberation', 'option for the poor') and blunted them by not accepting any of their structural implications.[2]

Concilium was bound up with the beginnings of liberation theology and the base communities. Over the last decade there has been a separate section for Third World Theology. However, liberation theology has had a voice not only here but in many contributions on universal theological questions. That will not change, but new challenges will be added, e.g. under social-ethical perspectives (Ethics and Lifestyles) and in the new area of Religion and Religious Experiences.

3. Asia

Marked processes of transformation are also taking place in Asia: religious, cultural and economic developments are tending on the one hand towards more plurality while on the other they are sharing in the process of globalization. Even if we note the difference between socialist constitutions, democracies with a market economy and still authoritarian structures, everywhere we can note new challenges from technological changes, a transformation in the forms of economies and new forms of communications. Asia has the highest proportion of so-called 'threshold countries' in the Two-Thirds World. In Asia many technological revolutions in digital and microbiological development encounter a cultural preparation for refined scientific and technological structures (e.g. in Japan) and reservations about Western individualization, even e.g. in the ethical basis of human rights. Collective and religious motives which transcend the individual, the notion of harmony with nature which is to be understood less in terms of opposition to manipulation than of a culture of embedding – all these are characteristics which need inter-cultural, inter-religious and inter-ethical understanding and development.

The problems arising from this relate to all the high religions present in Asia and therefore increasingly call for local inter-religious dialogue (such as has been carried on in *Concilium* especially by Aloysius Pieris and will also remain a commitment for the future). Here for the most part the church finds itself having a minority status. The voices of theology develop above all in regions with a marked Christian stamp. They are listened to all the more when they are combined with practical witnessing. The arrival of secularization and the mass media has not left the structure of the high religions untouched. Above all the political-religious units or balances have been disturbed. Their claims are often announced in a radicalized form from the political underground, which is integralist, intolerant and militant. Reflection on religious foundations is in a precarious situation as a result of the destruction of its political roots and resistance to the Western veneer consisting of a secular culture of televisions, refrigerators and Coca Cola. Fundamentalism is often regarded as a way out of the crisis of the high religions and as an alternative to the globalization of one-sided economic structures, but it does not practise sufficient differentiation. The religious, ethical and political dialogue has been strengthened by the future concentration of the areas of *Concilium*.

4. *Europe*[3]

The deficiencies in the situation of Christian faith, the loss of committed church members, the growing indifference of large groups of the population to 'metaphysical questions' and the return of the religious in the form of a 'supermarket' syncretism – all these things have often been described. But there are also new visions and opportunities: we can also note the new departure from thinking in terms of nation states in the direction of the processes of European integration; the discussion about the heritage of Central and Eastern Europe which is so varied; the many possibilities of alternative thinking in the framework of technological and economic developments including a grappling with capitalism robbed of its opposite pole, communism; ethnocentricity; religious integralism or sheer anarchic consumerism.

A living European theology and indeed the European churches no longer understand themselves 'centristically', i.e. at the centre of church universality and global theological efforts. Globalization and regionalizations are two sides of the same awareness. The experiences of this decentring has certainly not yet been sufficiently assimilated, especially as the decentring is going on in different directions. The great theological supermarket of North America has detached itself from Europe and come to understand itself less as an import than as an export concern. On the other hand, there is the new self-awareness of the theologies and churches of the Two-Thirds World, which has similarly set a great variety of learning processes in motion in Europe. The intercontinental exchange of theologies, above all in their various regional forms, continues to influence European theological thought and its new definition of this context in a way which has been fruitful. This definition of its context includes at least coming to terms with the European failure or the legacy of European domination (colonialism, imperialism, racism, secularism, etc.). What Martin Buber called 'reconciliation with oneself' after the Holocaust is still open. The challenge of secularity is being noted – the discussions about bioethics going on at many levels are a focal point here. Institutional religion, religious indifference and selective religious individualism clash and give rise to friction. Meanwhile the ecumenical dimension has come to be taken for granted, and it extends beyond Christian integration.

Tensions between academic Catholic theology and the church hierarchy are manifest. After the crisis in biblical studies and the crisis of dogmatics caused by the insights of science and historical research, the third crisis of modernism to develop has been the crisis in moral theology. This stems from coming to terms with the modern world, and the issues are more than detailed questions of sexual ethics and rules about contraception.

Constitutionally governed states and socialist states are one missionary option for Europe which in reality has constantly been lost. The crisis of the individual development of human rights and the collapse of social solidarity are new challenges for which old answers are as unsatisfactory as they are for the new ecological dimension of all social questions.

Concilium came into being in Europe and the new thinking of European theology in the Second Vatican Council (one might think of the founders: Yves Congar, Hans Küng, Karl Rahner and Edward Schillebeeckx). It has been administered in Europe but for a long time it has ceased to be made in Europe. Europeans appear among the theologians of *Concilium* who have been translated world-wide (like Johann Baptist Metz, Hans Küng and Jürgen Moltmann), but increasingly others are taking new ways (like Gustavo Gutierrez, Leonardo Boff, David Tracy, Elisabeth Schüssler Fiorenza, Aloysius Pieris). Here special emphasis should be placed on feminist theology, which since 1984 has had its own section in *Concilium*, now about to expand its 'Western' focal points by the sphere of 'Global Perspectives', especially on the question of God which influences not only inter-religious and ecumenical questions but also ethics. This is part of the vision of *Concilium*.

5. North America

Such a vision has gained a foothold above all in North America and has largely led to a greater involvement of women in theological activity. Much has changed fundamentally in the years since the Second Vatican Council, even if what Eugene Kennedy has described as 'Tomorrow's Catholics and Yesterday's Church' stand side by side in conflict and co-operation. North American theology has gained in international standing – and not just because of its large internal market, but also because of its involvement in the discussion of basic theological questions and in biblical criticism and dialogue with the cultures of our time; here the increasing influence of North America social philosophy also plays a part in Europe. The boom in so-called applied or practical ethics also stems from Anglo-Saxon philosophical culture, which is reacting more flexibly to the new technological challenges. Here, as in other spheres, theologians have succeeded in gaining a hearing in social discourse without their specific or even confessional origins playing a direct role. Theology works on bridging the gaps which separate it from its intellectual environment. Where the context is one of the study of religion the consequences are good; but Catholic theology in North America has also concerned itself with the question of the ecclesial nature of theology. Some dialogue papers which have attracted international attention have arisen from the controversy between the American bishops and the Roman magisterium.

All this also applies to the dialogical process in the discussion of social questions, which have become more pressing, and not just in North America. The revival of the prophetic elements of Christian social ethics over against an economism while rules as a substitute ethics has attracted critical attention. Here it has proved fruitful that the Catholic Church has been able to cultivate its independence in the minority and among minorities.

As can be read off its development, in the 1970s and 1980s *Concilium* increasingly turned towards North America, but without finding more than friendly respect as a universal enterprise in the narrow academic confines of the North American continent. The future will show whether co-operation can improve.

II Our common theological root

Concilium is bound up with the dawn ushered in by the Second Vatican Council. The hermeneutical key for all its work was to take up the pointers for the future which emerged from the Council. Therefore *Concilium* was able to develop further in the direction of Third World Theologies and Feminist Theology. Yet other focal points testify to the wealth of theology in the thirty years after the Council: ecumenical theology, political theology and liberation theology; the reading of the Bible by the church of the poor; the laying of theological foundations of new structures for the church; the hermeneutics of the signs of the time and narrative theology; the theology of religions; autonomous ethics in a Christian context.[4]

There have been so many ways, but there is only one source; there have been so many branches, but there is only one root: *our common theological root remains the question of God.* To many people in the Western world God seems to have become 'superfluous'. Such a statement can be interpreted in two divergent directions: God is either no more, or there is a superfluity of God. Both the disappearance, which is not even perceived as the emptying of a 'place', and the mass invasion of new diffuse or old integralist religion can be false theological expedients. But belief in a God who communicates himself, a liberating practice of remembrance which makes God present, and the dumb cry of human victims robbed of their individuality, all have a common root: what Nietzsche called the 'unquenched flame' of a fire which consumes itself in the need for God, fed by the recognition of one's own impotence and contingency, a fire which constantly keeps rekindling theological questions, often from apparently cold ashes.

III Many ways forward

1. We want to continue *ecumenical and conciliar processes* and find new ways for them. Alongside the ecumenical process in Christianity, which requires new efforts from us (e.g. in *Concilium* more non-Catholic directors) in view of the way in which it has got stuck, the practical conciliar process (Peace, Justice and the Preservation of Creation) has established itself, as have efforts to establish the common heritage of the Abrahamic religions, and finally world-wide inter-religious and inter-cultural dialogue and the social responsibility of the gospel. This is matched by:

2. *The prophetic political way.* A prophetic experience of contrast, a *concrete* negation of structural sins, arises out of the intensive encounter with God and the life of Jesus Christ. Its particular characteristic is that with its prophetic and mystical motif it can purge and relativize the *specific* negation, i.e. the negation which imprisons the negative from which it stems in the controversy and remains bound up with its fate. It is therefore creative. The negative by which it is provoked is the way into the creative vision of the future seen in revelation which is provided by the sources: the new creation (II Cor. 5.17), the new life, the new person, the new society.

This prophetic experience of contrast points specifically to commitment to human rights and the option for the poor, commitment to a living tradition in the *Concilium* movement.

3. *The way of women's liberation.* One of the most important prophetic experiences of contrast is the oppression of women, violence against women and sexism as the divide-and-rule method of a dominant androcentrism. The revival of a Christian tradition of the history of women which has been suppressed and marginalized, and a revision of the structures of church communion and office to make women visible, belong among the central concerns of *Concilium*. Women in the Bible and in the tradition of faith open up a history of liberation today which is reflected in a great cultural and religious variety. But the vision of the new society also lives on the stimuli provided by women's movements.

4. *The way of religious experience in Christianity and the Christian experience of the religious.* Religious experience and religious indifference are equally signs of our time, as are the demolition of religious institutions and the formation of religious movements. The religious *tremendum et facinosum* is both enlivening and ambiguous: ambiguous, because it needs enlightenment by reason, but also because what is Christian does not just manifest itself in religious forms nor is it exhausted by them. Here at the same time *Concilium* stands for a revival or deepening of religious experience and for a discernment of the spirits.

5. *The way of the one world.* A move towards globalization is necessary and indispensable. The problems of the viability of the earth and ecological equilibrium, the concern for peace and the just distribution of resources, are problems of global dimension which call for a new global thought in all areas and all dimensions of life. Here questions are raised about the right institutions, about ethics and law. Here questions also arise constantly about co-operation between religions, the controversy with integralisms and fundamentalisms, but also of the world vision of 'Christianity' which regards God as the 'mystery of the world', to use Eberhard Jüngel's phrase. The globalization of hermeneutical questions in theology also calls for new efforts.

6. *The way of regional bases.* The more global we are, the more regional we shall become. This new dialectic, in accordance with which every step towards globalization will be bound up with another step towards the intensification of regional peculiarities in order to find a balance, must be observed. There can be no globalization without a corresponding solidarity, or without a corresponding subsidiarity. At the same time that calls for a renunciation of centralistic intellectual figures and global concentrations of power. It also means a strengthening of dialogical learning processes and equal rights for regions and cultures.

7. *The way of communities.* Without tangible living communities which significantly differ from one another in their plurality, putting into action the idea of the positive competition of successful forms of life, and recalling the commitment symbolized by the gospel, there can be neither living churches nor structures of common life which are worthy of human beings. *Concilium* has always lived by communities, e.g. religious communities and base communities. This must have a marked and rich continuation.

8. *The way of scholarship and interdisciplinary work.* A commitment to scholarship, to scholarly communication and to scholarly innovation is taken for granted by a journal which embraces the whole theological spectrum and in this sense understands itself as a theological journal. However, here different regional profiles are developing which must continue to dialogue with one another. Furthermore theology, which in any case lives by the integration of quite different individual methods, must strengthen its interdisciplinary nature and constantly measure itself by the levels attained in other academic disciplines.

9. *A creative conscience and the need for participation.* The challenges of ethical responsibility are important not only for global problems (see above, 3.5) but also for forms of life and life-styles. The question of the good life or the success and good fortune of human life in its various spheres, at its various stages, and in its different relationships is a central question of the development of ethical autonomy (i.e. free commitment) and solidarity. The concept of conscience has become central to this creative responsibility of the individual in his or her life, and also in church and society. Conscience plays a part in the criticism, shaping and preservation of social institutions through participation in scholarship and a corresponding critical and constructive openness. Participation is the necessary context of freedom of conscience. It presupposes conditions of democratic freedom, especially the sharing of power. This is contradicted by particular jurisdictional structures and actual conditions of power in the churches and in society. In its history *Concilium* has always fought for such a critical consciousness and for the changes in the church which that necessitates. This will also be a central project in the future.

10. *The way of suffering men and women towards the question of the grounds for our hope.* The suffering and dying, the exploited and marginalized, are an oppressive sign of our time. Those of us whose conscience has not yet been blunted are oppressed above all by the anonymous torment of the infinite numbers of such people. The cry of the poor is as little noticed as the fate of those who are scarcely born before their breath is quenched, whose existence is barely perceived except in the dumb dismay in the eyes of their mothers. This

sign is called the 'rock of atheism'. Whereas in the centuries of the 'Enlightenment' the failure of God to respond was experienced by many people as the tremendous mystery of a mystical withdrawal, and to the end religion was thought to be indestructible, as a 'praxis for overcoming contingency', and an attempt was made to take refuge in a faith which was unthematic intuition and supposition, these are not appropriate models for a hope based on faith in the self-communication of God. However great the distance may be between a consumerist-practical atheism in the modern world and an atheism which is 'mystical' or born out of theodicy, they unite as a paralysing sign of a remoteness from religion which goes hand in hand with an individual quest to meet religious need along with the aggressive self-assertion of a declamatory religious fanaticism. The question of the ground for our hope in the face of such signs leads directly to the central foundation of the ways to the common theological root which have been described here. This question will continue to motivate and unsettle the work of the theologians of *Concilium*, and will mean that there will be no satisfied or satiated theology in *Concilium* and its circle. Rather, the concern will be a theology of liberation which is driven by the varied impulses of movements for freedom, peace and justice while at the same time drinking from its source in revelation history. The basic word 'liberation' has long accompanied and renewed the word *Concilium* in our international journal for theology. God's love has chosen the way of freedom which does not seek to dominate but to entrance, so as finally to embrace beloved and freed men and women in its arms.

IV The common criterion: Jesus Christ

Christianity tells of its prophet Jesus of Nazareth as a divine-human figure who provides verification, i.e. as a historical form of life in whom the history of God and the history of humankind fuse into one. This event is all the more provocative as it comes to be concentrated in images which gather around the historical event of Jesus' death on the cross, and which at least contain as much shock as comfort. The cross is one of the worst inventions of human cruelty. In times when death is so visibly a part of daily life that merely inflicting it has no terrors, human beings will be particularly inventive in the instruments of torture they use to assert their power. The cross is a symbol for exaltation and humiliation at the same time. It is an excess of evil as an expression of human self-empowerment. It remains a provocation that God is said to be at home as the victim where human beings slaughter other human beings. However, for Christians the cross can be made a symbol only when it is regarded as the expression of the consequences of a life story. Detached from the biography of Jesus of Nazareth it can be made nonsensical, as can be seen from the Christian Crusades, which can only be interpreted as a great abuse of memory in the name of power. The crucified Jesus is a human being who does not fight the failure of human beings in their self-empowerment with the same means of power, but rather introduces his divine authority into human powerlessness. But precisely in so doing he breaks the continuity of evil. Any other battle is stamped by the negative which it fights. Any counter power adopts the means of power with which it is fighting. The impotence of the God-man assumed in the fate of the cross is different. It is an interruption of the history of sin and the birthplace of new forms of life which are impotent but liberating.

Similarly, the life of Jesus told by the Gospels in different ways remains a criterion for the event of the resurrection, witness to which is the foundation of the apostolic church. For the life of Jesus and his own testimony to life is so strong that the disciples cannot believe that his crucifixion was the end. The resurrection is first of all the resurrection of their faith, after it had to withstand the searing test of the crucifixion. Any concentration of the Christian in abstract conceptual statements must be brought back to the narrated form of the life of Jesus of Nazareth. For here we have the criterion for the correct interpretation of the cross, for the understanding of the resurrection and finally also for the 'Spirit' which revives a failed faith. The Christian tradition understands this history as a history of knowledge and a history of love. The history of knowledge can also be summarized in the word 'revelation'. The Spirit as the ever-ongoing presence of the divine in love gives a valid stamp to the forms of life which understand themselves as testimony to the Christian revelation. These forms of life must be spoken of adequately if what is Christian in Christianity is to be clarified.

Notes

1. For the following analyses of Africa, Latin America and Asia, which are certainly very generalized, I am indebted to Peter Hünermann, since August 1996 President of the International Network of Societies for Catholic Theology.

2. For the danger of a commandeering of liberation theology, above all by neo-liberalism, see Franz J. Hinkelammert, 'Über den Markt zum Reich Gottes?', *Orientierung* 60, 1996, 98–102, 115–20.

3. For the remarks on Europe and North America see Dietmar Mieth, 'Theologie, Profile und Enwicklungstendenzen im internationlen Umfeld', in *Forschungpolitische Früherkennung*, produced by the Schweizerischer Wissenschaftsrat in Bern, 156/1995; also in *Bulletin der Europäischen Gesellschaft für Katholische Theologie* 7, 1996.

4. For some developments see Rosino Gibellini, *La teologica del XX secolo*, Brescia 1992; cf. also D. Mieth, E. Schillebeeckx and D. Snijdewind (eds.), *Aufbruch und Vision, Universitalität und Regionalität der Theologie im 20. Jahrhundert*, Brescia 1996.

Contributors

KARL-JOSEF KUSCHEL was born in 1948. He studied German and theology at the universities of Bochum and Tübingen. He did his doctoral studies in Tübingen, where he was an academic assistant, and from 1981 to 1995 worked at the Institute for Ecumenical Research and Catholic Faculty there. He is now Professor of Culture and Inter-Religious Dialogue in the University of Tübingen. As well as editing many works, he has written *Jesus in der deutschsprächigen Gegenwartsliteratur* (1978); *Heute noch knien? Über ein Bild von Edouard Manet* (1979); *Stellvertreter Christi? Der Papst in der zeitgenössischen Literatur* (1980); *Gottesbilder-Menschenbilder. Blicke durch die Literatur unserer Zeit* (1985); *Weil wir uns auf dieser Erde nicht ganz zu Hause fühlen. Zwölf Schriftsteller über Religion und Literatur* (1985); *Born Before All Time: The Dispute over Christ's Origin* (1992); *Laughter: A Theological Reflection* (1994); *Abraham: A Symbol of Hope for Jews, Christians and Muslims* (1995).

Address: Sandäckerstrasse 2, 72070 Tübingen, Germany.

NORBERT METTE was born in Barkhausen/porta, Germany in 1946. After studying theology and sociology he gained a doctorate in theology, and since 1984 he has been Professor of Practical Theology at the University of Paderborn. He is married with three children. He has written numerous works on pastoral theology and religious education, including: *Voraussetzungen christlicher Elementarerziehung* (1983); *Kirche auf dem Weg ins Jahr 2000* (with M. Blasberg-Kuhnke, 1986); *Gemeindepraxis in Grundbegriffen* (with C. Bäumler, 1987); *Auf der Seite der Unterdrückten? Theologie der Befreiung im Kontext Europas* (ed. with P. Eicher, 1989); *Der Pastorale Notstand* (with O. Fuchs, 1992); *Religionspädagogik* (1994).

Address: Liebigweg 11a, D48165 Münster, Germany.

CRISTINA GRENHOLM was born in 1959; she is Assistant Professor in Studies in Faiths and Ideologies at the Theological Faculty of Uppsala University. She was ordained in the Church of Sweden in 1985. She finished her doctoral dissertation in 1990 and has remained at the Theological Faculty of Uppsala since then. In 1992 she was awarded the Oscar Prize of Uppsala University (named after King Oscar II) for her theological research. She has published many academic and popular articles and reviews on the topics of biblical exegesis and systematic theology, Christian interpretation of the Old Testament, contemporary theology and feminist theology.

Address: Heimdalsvägen 12, S-756 52 Uppsala, Sweden.

SEAN FREYNE is currently Professor of Theology at Trinity College, Dublin, having previously lectured on Biblical Studies in the USA and Australia. His theological and biblical studies were completed at St Patrick's College, Maynooth, Ireland; the Biblical Institute, Rome; and the Institutum Judaicum of the University of Tübingen, West Germany. He is the author of a number of books and articles on Second Temple Judaism and Early Christianity, most recently, *Galilee, Jesus and the Gospels. Literary Approaches and Historical Investigations* (1988). He joined the editorial board of *Concilium* in 1987 and is also currently on the editorial board of *New Testament Studies*.

Address: 24 Charleville Road, Dublin 6, Ireland.

JOSEPH MOINGT was born in 1915 and became a Jesuit in 1939. He was Professor of Systematic Theology successively at the Jesuit Faculty of Lyons-Fourvière and then at the Catholic Institute of Paris, and now holds that post at the Jesuit Faculty of the Sèvres Centre in Paris. He has been editor of *Recherches de Science religieuse* since 1968. His most recent book is *L'homme qui venait de Dieu*, Paris 1993.

Address: 15 rue Monsieur, 75007 Paris, France.

PIERRE GISEL was born in Geneva in 1947 and after a pastorate became Professor of Systematic Theology in the University of Lausanne, a post which he has now held for twenty years. His books include *Vérité et Histoire* (on Käsemann), Paris ²1983; *La Création*, Geneva ²1987; *Croyance incarnée*, Geneva 1986; *Le Christ de Calvin*, Paris 1990; *Corps et esprit*, Geneva 1992; *La subversion de l'Esprit*, Geneva 1993; *Pourquoi baptiser?*, Geneva 1994. He is also editor of the monumental *Encyclopédie du protestantisme*, Paris and Geneva 1995.

Address: Université de Lausanne, Faculté de Théologie, BFSH2–1015 Lausanne, Switzerland.

RICHARD G. COTE, an American Oblate missionary, is Associate Professor of Mission Studies at Saint Paul University in Ottawa. He holds degrees from the Catholic University of Angers, and earned his doctorate in Religious Studies at the University of Strasbourg. An Advisory Committee member of and contributor to *Concilium*, he is author of *Universal Grace: Myth or Reality?* and a forthcoming book, *Re-Visioning Mission: The Catholic Church and Culture in Postmodern America*.

Address: Saint Paul University, 223 Main Street, Ottawa, ON K1S 1C5, Canada.

JOHN K. RICHES is Professor of Divinity and Biblical Criticism in the University of Glasgow, Scotland. He is the author of *Jesus and the Transformation of Judaism* (1980), *The World of Jesus* (1990) and *A Century of New Testament Study* (1993). He is a priest of the Scottish Episcopal Church, a member of the International Anglican-Orthodox Theological Dialogue, and has a practical involvement in a small development trust which promotes alternative trading. His own research interests are in studies of the historical Jesus and first-century Judaism and in theological interpretation of the New Testament. With Justin Ukpong of the Catholic Institute of West Africa he initiated a project on *The Bible in African Contexts*. This has also led to co-operation on methods of Contextual Bible Study with the Institute for the Study of the Bible in Pietermaritzburg. He is presently engaged on a study of modes of self-identification in the New Testament.

Address: The University of Glasgow, Dept. of Biblical Studies, Glasgow G12 8QQ, Scotland.

ANNE FORTIN-MELKEVIK was born in Quebec in 1957 and studied theology there. She gained a doctorate in religious anthropology and the history of religions at the Sorbonne and a doctorate in theology at the Institut Catholique in 1991 on 'A Rational Theory of Hermeneutics in

Theology'. Since then she has taught fundamental theology and christology at the Faculty of Theology of the Université Laval of Quebec.

Address: Faculté de théologie, Université Laval, Québec, Canada G1K 7P4.

RENÉ KIEFFER was born at Aumetz in 1930 and lived in Luxembourg from 1934 to 1956. From 1955 to 1962 he studied philosophy and languages in Paris, Freiburg in Breisgau and Munich (gaining a doctorate in Luxembourg), and philosophy and theology at the Dominican faculty Le Saulchoir, where he was a lecturer; he gained a diploma at the École Biblique in Jerusalem. Since 1965 he has lived in Sweden and in 1968 gained a doctorate in New Testament at Uppsala. He was lecturer at Lund from 1970 to 1989 and since 1990 has been professor at Uppsala. His main interests are John, Paul and linguistic analysis. He has written in Swedish a theology of the New Testament and a commentary on St John in two volumes.

Address: Paprikagaan 3, 75449 Uppsala, Sweden.

EDMUND ARENS was born in Lemathe, Germany in 1953. He studied theology and philosophy in the Catholic faculties at Münster and Frankfurt, gaining his doctorate in 1982. In 1989 he became a lecturer at the University of Münster and in 1996 was appointed Professor of Fundamental Theology at the Hochschule in Luzern. His publications include *The Logic of Pragmatic Thinking*, 1994; *Bezeugen und Bekennen. Elementare Handlungen des Glaubens*, 1989; *Christopraxis*, 1995.

Address: Diesterwegstrasse 23, D 60594 Frankfurt am Main, Germany.

MARY GREY was born in the north of England in 1941 and studied at Oxford (Classics and Philosophy) and at the Catholic University of Louvain, Belgium. For five years she was Professor of Feminism and Christendom at the Catholic University of Nijmegen, The Netherlands, and is now Professor of Contemporary Theology at the University of Southampton (La Sainte Union College). She writes and lectures in Feminist Liberation Theology and co-ordinated the European delegation to the EATWOT dialogue of women theologians in Costa Rica in 1994, 'Women Struggling against Global Violence: A Spirituality for Life'. She edits the journal *Ecotheology* – formerly *Theology in Green*, and among other publications has written *Redeeming the Dream* (1989), on redemption, and *The Wisdom of Fools?* (1993), on revelation. She is current engaged with ecclesiology from a feminist liberationist and ecological perspective. With her husband Nicholas Grey she set up a charity, Wells for India, and is involved in social work in Rajasthan.

Address: LSU College, University of Southampton, The Avenue, Southampton SO17 1BG, UK.

Concilium 1997/1

The editors wish to thank the great number of colleagues from the various Advisory Committees who contributed in a most helpful way to the final project.

Rafael Aguirre	Bilbao	Spain
Marcella Althaus-Reid	Edinburgh	Scotland
Alberto Antoniazzi	Belo Horizonte	Brasil
Maria Pilar Aquino	San Diego	USA
Edmund Arens	Frankfurt	Germany
José Arguello	Managua	Nicaragua
Anne Carr	Chicago	USA
Richard Cote OMI	Ottawa	Canada
Helena Czosnyka	St Louis	USA
Wanda Deifelt	Sao Leopoldo	Brasil
Karl Derksen OP	Utrecht	The Netherlands
Monique Dumais	Rimouski	Canada
Felisa Elizondo Aragón	Madrid	Spain
Edward Farrugia	Rome	Italy
Irmtraud Fischer	Graz	Austria
David Ford	Cambridge	Great Britain
Ann Fortin-Melkevik	Laval	Canada
Ottmar Fuchs	Bamberg	Germany
Alexandre Ganoczy	Würzburg	Germany
Pierre Gisel	Lausanne	Switzerland
Mary Grey	Southampton	Great Britain
Thomas Groome	Boston	USA
Frans Haarsma	Nijmegen	The Netherlands
Ferdinand Heselaars-Harono SJ	Yogyakarta	Indonesia
Mary Hunt	Silver Spring	USA
Anne Jensen	Tübingen	Germany
Ottmar John	Ibbenbüren	Germany
Hubert Lepargneur OP	Sao Paulo	Brasil
Norbert Mette	Münster	Germany
Josef Meyer zu Schlochtern	Gelsenkirchen	Germany
Hedwig Meyer-Wilmes	Nijmegen	The Netherlands
Ronald Modras	St Louis	USA
Emmanuel Ntakarutimana	Budjumbura	Burundi

Teresa Okure	Port Harcourt	Nigeria
Matthew Paikada	Kerala	India
Raimundo Panikkar	Barcelona	Spain
Otto Hermann Pesch	Hamburg	Germany
John Riches	Glasgow	Great Britain
Herwi Rikhof	Nijmegen	The Netherlands
Hermann Rüegger	Bern	Switzerland
P. Samir Khalil	Paris	France
Heinz Robert Schlette	Bonn	Germany
Robert Schreiter CPPS	Chicago	USA
Silvia Schroer	Köniz	Switzerland
Sidbe Sempord	Cotonou	Rep. of Benin
†George M. Soares Prabhu SJ	Ramwadi Pune	India
Regula Strobel	Freiburg	Switzerland
Paolo Suess	Sao Paulo	Brasil
Leonard Swidler	Philadelphia	USA
Stephen Sykes	Cambridge	Great Britain
John Edwin Thiel	Fairfield	USA
Justin Ukpong	Port Harcourt	Nigeria
Bas van Iersel SMM	Nijmegen	The Netherlands
Jerome Walsh	Jackson Heights	USA

We also wish to express our gratitude to three persons from the Association for Practical Theology in Indonesia, who received our Provisional Project in the Indonesian language through Ferninand Heselaars Harono SJ:

John Mansford Prior	Maumere	Indonesia
Mathias Yamrewav	Yogyakarta	Indonesia
Siegfried Zahnweh SJ	Klepu-Semarang	Indonesia